NEW EDITION

1

LADO ENGLISH SERIES

Robert Lado

Professor of Linguistics Emeritus and Former Dean
School of Languages and Linguistics
Georgetown University

Former Director
English Language Institute
University of Michigan

in collaboration with

JEROME C. FORD   BERNADETTE SHERIDAN, I.H.M.

LARRY ANGER   ANNETTE SILVERIO-BORGES

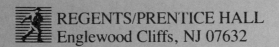

REGENTS/PRENTICE HALL
Englewood Cliffs, NJ 07632

Editorial/production supervision: Louisa B. Hellegers
Editorial development: Louis Carrillo/Bill Preston
Interior design/page layout: A Good Thing Inc.
Design supervision: Janet Schmid
Manufacturing buyer: Laura Crossland

Cover design: Janet Schmid
Cover photograph: © Slide Graphics of New England, Inc.

Illustrations by Silvio Redinger
Maps and illustrations on pages 119 and 123 by Anna Divito

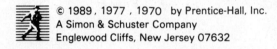
Printed in the United States of America

10 9 8 7 6

ISBN 0-13-522244-3

Prentice-Hall International (UK) Limited, *London*
Prentice-Hall of Australia Pty. Limited, *Sydney*
Prentice-Hall Canada Inc., *Toronto*
Prentice-Hall Hispanoamericana, S.A., *Mexico*
Prentice-Hall of India Private Limited, *New Delhi*
Prentice-Hall of Japan, Inc., *Tokyo*
Simon & Schuster Asia Pte. Ltd., *Singapore*
Editora Prentice-Hall do Brasil, Ltda., *Rio de Janeiro*

CONTENTS

PREFACE

The new edition of the *Lado English Series* is a complete six-level course in English. Each level is carefully graded and consists of a Student Book, Workbook, Teacher's Edition, and Audio Program. The main objective of the series is to help students understand, speak, read, and write English and to use these four skills for meaningful communication and interaction.

The new *Lado English Series* takes a balanced approach to teaching and learning. It offers a wide variety of techniques and activities—including conversations and discussions, study frames and contextualized grammar exercises, listening and interaction activities, readings and role plays—to help students learn English. The more controlled, structured exercises focus attention on learning the grammatical rules of English, while the freer, open-ended activities offer ways of improving language skills through more creative, spontaneous interaction.

This new edition retains the careful grading, simple presentation, and transparent organization that are classic trademarks of the *Lado English Series*. At the same time, several new features make this edition more modern and easy to use. The revised Student Book format features a larger type size, bigger pages, updated and extended content, and new art. For greater convenience, the Listening sections have been moved from the Workbooks to the Student Books. Cassette symbols appear throughout the Student Books to identify recorded material.

The exercises in the six Workbooks correspond to and complement the material covered in the Student Books. They offer additional exercises to help students master the material in each unit and focus on vocabulary, reading, and writing. In this new edition, controlled composition appears in all six Workbooks. In addition, review units with pre- and post-inventory Tests are now included at the end of each Workbook.

The Teacher's Editions have been revised and reformatted. The new horizontal page format features clear, concise instructions. For easy reference, these instructions appear in single columns on each page of the Teacher's Edition and face a nearly full-size reproduction of the corresponding page from the Student Book. The answers to all the exercises are given together with the reproduced page. New vocabulary presented in the unit is listed at the beginning of each section. This is followed by a concise explanation of how to teach the section. Suggestions for games are also given, so that students have the opportunity to use English in less formal situations. Answers to all Workbook exercises can be found in an answer key at the back of the Teacher's Edition.

An Audio Program for each level consists of five cassettes corresponding to each Student Book. The program gives students the opportunity to listen to native speech, and can be used outside of class to provide extra speaking and listening practice.

By offering a combination of grammatical and functional activities, Student Book 1 helps students achieve accuracy and build effective communication skills. The Conversation and Interaction sections allow students to use English more naturally and functionally before they focus on particular language structures in the Study and Practice sections that follow. Thus, students work with both the function (use) and the grammatical form (structure) of English.

Student Book 1 has ten units. These units are divided into sections with clear headings that indicate the purpose of the sections: Conversation, Interaction, Study, Practice, Listen, Speak, Read, Think, and Pronounce. Following are guidelines for presenting the material in each unit.

Each unit opens with a **Conversation** that introduces the new material in a communicative setting. Pictures help to set the context. Intonation lines show the rise and fall of the voice. They represent the four intonation levels of English: low, mid, high, and extra high. A dot on the intonation line indicates the principal stress in each sentence.

- Describe the situation while students look at the pictures.
- Explain any new or unfamiliar vocabulary or structures.
- Read the conversation while students follow along in their books.
- Assign each role to a part of the class. Read the conversation and have the students repeat the lines that correspond to their roles.
- Assign each role to an individual student. Read the conversation and have the students repeat the lines that correspond to their roles.
- Divide the class into pairs or small groups and have the students practice the conversation.
- Ask a group to present the conversation in front of the class.

In the **Interaction** section, students adapt the opening conversation to new situations by modifying significant parts of the dialogue with the help of cues. Some Interaction sections contain an additional application step (see Teacher's Edition), in which students create more personal exchanges that give information about themselves.

- Read the cues; then read the sentences. Have students repeat the sentences after you.
- Read the cues. Have two students read the sentences.
- Read the cues (or have a student read them). Have two students make the sentences.

You may want to practice the Interaction using a group or individual approach. For the group approach, divide the class into two groups and have one group ask the questions for the other group to answer. For the individual approach, call on an individual student to form the question and direct it to another student for the answer.

The **Study** sections present grammatical structures in a clear, graphic way. Study frames have been redone in the new edition, with boxes, connecting lines, and illustrations updated to make the grammatical relationships clearer.

- Read the examples while students follow along in their books.
- Explain the structure(s), using the example sentences and illustrations.
- Give further examples of the structure to ensure student comprehension.

A **Practice** section follows each Study frame. This section contains exercises which allow students to use the target grammar in meaningful contexts. Many exercises include an additional application step (see Teacher's edition), in which students personalize the structures by giving information about themselves.

- Explain any new or unfamiliar vocabulary.
- Present the example to the class. Check for comprehension.
- Have students do the exercises.

The **Listen** section contains any of three types of exercises, all of which require students to listen to sentences, dialogues, and paragraphs and then indicate the correct choices or fill in the blanks. The exercises can be used for listening practice or for listening comprehension tests. All exercises are included on the audio cassettes available for each level of the series.

- If you are using the exercises for listening practice, read (or play) each item twice and let the students respond.
- If you are using them for tests, read or play the items only once.
- After students have completed each exercise, write the correct responses on the board so that they can check their work.

In the **Speak** section, students use newly learned vocabulary and grammar in a variety of more creative situations. Students focus on reading and performing dialogues, not on memorizing them. Students also modify the dialogues by using cues in the text to express information about themselves.

- Explain any new or unfamiliar vocabulary.
- Read the conversation in part A while students follow along.
- Have two students perform the conversation.
- With books open, ask two students to perform the conversation in part B using the cues. Repeat this step with other students.
- For another variation, have two students perform the conversation with their books closed. Repeat this step with other students.

The **Read** section contains short passages composed of material presented in the unit. Questions follow each reading to check comprehension and stimulate discussion. Reading becomes increasingly emphasized as a language skill as students work through the series.

- Explain any new or unfamiliar vocabulary.
- Have the students read the text silently, using the illustration to help them understand the content.
- Ask students to work in pairs and ask and answer the questions. If students do not agree on an answer, have them return to the reading passage to resolve their disagreement.

The **Think** section gives students another opportunity to use English in a less-controlled, more communicative way. The pictures in this section encourage students to use new structures and vocabulary more freely and creatively.

- Ask students to look at and think about the illustrations. Help them with vocabulary if necessary.
- Have students talk about the illustrations, preferably in pairs or small groups.
- Encourage students to relate their own experiences to the situation(s) if appropriate.

The **Pronounce** section focuses on particular elements of pronunciation that may cause problems in understanding and speaking English. Throughout the series, the Pronounce sections progressively treat all the phonemes of English; they also deal with consonant clusters and other aspects of pronunciation unique to English spelling, stress, and intonation. In many cases, facial diagrams are included to illustrate the articulation of particular sounds.

- Point out the key word and picture with the featured sound, facial diagram (if there is one), familiar words, and sentences containing the sound.
- Pronounce the words (or play the appropriate cassette) and have students practice saying them.
- You may want to have students practice pronouncing minimal pairs—two words in which all sounds but one are identical (for example, *sheep* and *ship*.)
- To provide practice in pronouncing featured sounds in a larger context, ask the students first to read aloud each of the sentences individually; then have them say the whole group of sentences.

This new edition offers a complete and balanced program for teaching and learning the structures and functions of English. Hopefully, the new features and design will make the series even more appealing, convenient, and effective for promoting learning and communication.

ROBERT LADO
Washington, D.C.

CONVERSATION

Introducing a Friend

BILL: Linda, this is Philip.

Philip is a student.

He's American.

LINDA: Nice to meet you, Philip.

PHILIP: Nice to meet you, too.

BILL: Linda is a tourist.

She's Chinese.

INTERACTION

A. Make sentences like the models.

EX. Linda, **this is Philip.**
Nice to meet you, Philip.
Nice to meet you, too.

1. Bill, _____.
_____, Rosa.
_____, too.

2. Julia, _____.
_____, Victor.
_____, too.

3. Albert, _____.
_____, Carolyn.
_____, too.

4. Carmen, _____.
_____, Toshi.
_____, too.

5. Introduce two classmates.

B. Make sentences like the models. Use the word cues.

EX. Philip/student.
American.
  ⇩ **Philip is a student.**
  He's American.

1. Bill/salesman.
English.
  ⇩

2. Aki/doctor.
Japanese.
  ⇩

3. Albert/tourist.
French.
  ⇩

4. Linda/tourist.
Chinese.
  ⇩

5. Yoko/secretary.
Japanese.
  ⇩

6. Julia/doctor.
Brazilian.
  ⇩

7. Tell about your
classmates.
  ⇩

STUDY 1

Affirmative statements: *Philip is a student.*

Notice the noun phrase and the verb phrase.

This	is Philip.
Philip	is a student.
He	's American.
This	is Linda.
Linda	is Chinese.
She	's a tourist.

He's is the contraction of **he is**.
She's is the contraction of **she is**.
Use the contractions in conversation.

 # PRACTICE

Make sentences like the models. Use the cues.

EX. Linda.
　　 tourist.
　　 Chinese.
　▷ **This is Linda.**
　　 She's a tourist.
　　 She's Chinese.

 Linda

 China

1. Carolyn.
　　 teacher.
　　 American.

　▷

 Carolyn

 United States

2. Victor.
doctor.
Colombian.

Victor Colombia

3. Rosa.
saleswoman.
Italian.

Rosa Italy

4. Oscar.
teacher.
Puerto Rican.

Oscar Puerto Rico

5. Monique.
scientist.
French.

Monique France

6. Manuel.
mechanic.
Venezuelan.

Manuel Venezuela

7. Introduce a classmate.

STUDY 2

Yes-no questions with **is**: *Is Philip in class?*

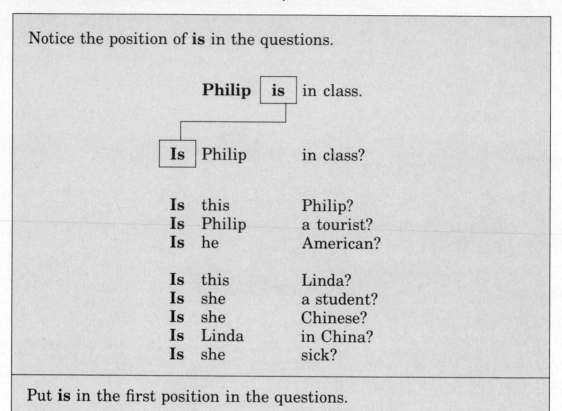

Notice the position of **is** in the questions.

Philip | **is** | in class.

Is | Philip | in class?

Is	this	Philip?
Is	Philip	a tourist?
Is	he	American?

Is	this	Linda?
Is	she	a student?
Is	she	Chinese?
Is	Linda	in China?
Is	she	sick?

Put **is** in the first position in the questions.

[cassette icon] # PRACTICE

A. Ask and answer questions.

EX. Philip/tall?
     short.
  ⇨ **Is Philip tall?**
     No. He's short.
     Bill is tall.

Bill   Philip

1. Linda/sad?
    happy.

    ⇨

    Linda   Yoko

2. Mary/present?
    absent.

    ⇨

    Lynn   Mary

3. Victor/sick?
    fine.

    ⇨

    Victor   John

4. Somsak/old?
    young.

    ⇨

    Somsak   Louise

5. Robert/right?
    wrong.

    ⇨

    2+2=4   2+2=6

    Rosa   Robert

6. Ask about a classmate.

    ⇨

8

B. Ask yes-no questions using the cues. Look at the pictures and answer the questions.

EX. Bill?
    a student?
  ▷ **Is this Bill?**
    No. This is Philip.
    Is he a student?
    Yes. He's a student.

1. Jim?
   young?
  ▷

2. Vanh?
   sick?
  ▷

3. Mary?
   a student?
  ▷

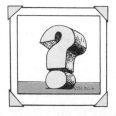

4. Alice?
   tall?
  ▷

5. Ask about a classmate.
  ▷

LISTEN

A. Look at the pictures below. Then listen to each sentence and write the letter of the sentence next to the matching picture.

1. _____

2. _____

3. _____

4. _____

5. _____

6. _____

B. Listen to each question. Then choose the correct answer.

1. a. No. She's Chinese.
   b. No. She's fine.
   c. Yes. She's a student.
2. a. Yes. She's a doctor.
   b. Yes. He's fine.
   c. No. He's a teacher.
3. a. Yes. He's English.
   b. Yes. He's a student.
   c. Yes. He's in class.
4. a. No. She's a nurse.
   b. Yes. She's absent.
   c. Yes. She's in class.
5. a. Yes. He's American.
   b. Yes. He's a student.
   c. Yes. He's a tourist.
6. a. No. He's in class.
   b. Yes. She's absent.
   c. Yes. She's in class.

SPEAK

A. Look at the map and listen to the conversation.

    BILL: This is Philip.

LINDA: Is he Canadian?

    BILL: No. He's American.

LINDA: Is he in the United States?

    BILL: Yes. He's in New York.

B. Practice the conversation with a classmate. Point to people on the map and ask about them.

STUDENT 1:   This is _____.

STUDENT 2:   Is he (she) _____?

STUDENT 1:   No. He's (She's) _____.

STUDENT 2:   Is he (she) in _____?

STUDENT 1:   Yes. He's (She's) in _____.

C. Now cover up parts A and B and look at the map. Practice the conversation with a different classmate.

CANADA

Philip

UNITED STATES

Ottawa

Linda

Chicago

San Francisco

New York

Washington, D.C.

Oscar

Miami

MEXICO

Havana

JAMAICA

HAITI

Ramón

Mexico City

CUBA

DOMINICAN REPUBLIC

Puerto Rico

BELIZE

HONDURAS

GUATEMALA

EL SALVADOR

NICARAGUA

VENEZUELA

Manuel

COSTA RICA

GUYANA

PANAMA

SURINAM

FRENCH GUIANA

Caracas

Victor

COLOMBIA

Bogotá

Guayaquil

ECUADOR

BRAZIL

Julia

PERU

Brasilia

Lima

Carmen

La Paz

BOLIVIA

Rio de Janeiro

PARAGUAY

São Paolo

Asunción

CHILE

URUGUAY

Santiago

Montevideo

Buenos Aires

ARGENTINA

READ

A. Read the items below. Then match them with the pictures.

a

b

c

d

_____1. This is a hospital in the United States. It's in New York City. It's old.

_____2. This is Mary Wilson. She's American. She's sick. She's in this hospital.

_____3. This is Alice Garcia. She's American, too. She's a nurse in this hospital.

_____4. This is Alan Wong. He's a doctor in this hospital. Dr. Wong is Chinese.

B. Ask and answer the questions.

1. Is this hospital old?
2. Is it in San Francisco?
3. Is Mary sick?
4. Is she in class?

C. Ask questions about Alice Garcia and Alan Wong.

THINK

Look at the picture of the math class. Ask and answer yes-no questions. Use the words below.

doctor   in class   absent   wrong

sick   present   teacher   friend

EX. Is Carolyn Jackson a doctor?
  ⇩ **No. She's a teacher.**

    Is Donald in class?
  ⇩ **Yes. He's in class.**

PRONOUNCE: [i]

ship	front, open, lax
	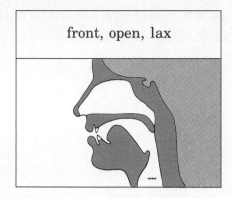

A. Repeat the words.

this	Linda	Alice	Bill
Victor	Philip	**English**	is

B. Repeat the sentences.

1. Is this a ship?
   Yes. This is a ship.

2. Is this Bill?
   No. This is Philip.

 Philip

3. Is this Alice?
   No. This is Linda.

 Linda

C. On a sheet of paper, write the numbers of the words that have the sound [i].

1. this	5. is	9. Bill	13. ship
2. Linda	6. friend	10. student	14. Wilson
3. fine	7. English	11. Victor	15. England
4. sick	8. nice	12. in	16. Chinese

CONVERSATION

Getting Acquainted

JIM: Hi, Philip.

PHILIP: Hello, Jim.

LINDA: Are you and Jim friends?

PHILIP: No. We're brothers.

LINDA: Really? Jim is very tall!

PHILIP: Yes. He's tall and I'm short.

LINDA: What about your father?

Is he tall or short?

PHILIP: He's tall. My mother is tall, too.

INTERACTION

A. Make sentences like the models. Use the word cues.

EX. Jim/friends?
brothers.

⇨ Are you and Jim friends?
No. We're brothers.
Really?
Yes.

1. Mai Li/sisters?
cousins.

⇨

2. Linda/brother and sister?
friends.

⇨

3. Oscar/mechanics?
teachers.

⇨

4. Julia/nurses?
doctors.

⇨

5. Somsak/friends?
brother and sister.

⇨

6. your friend/teachers?
students.

⇨

B. Make sentences like the models. Use the cues.

EX.   father?   ▷ **What about your father?**
      tall/short?   **Is he tall or short?**
      short.   **He's short.**

1.   father?   ▷
     a teacher/a doctor?
     a doctor.

2.   mother?   ▷
     a doctor/a scientist?
     a scientist.

3.   cousin?   ▷
     short/tall?
     tall.

4.   brother?   ▷
     present/absent?
     absent.

5.   father?   ▷
     old/young?
     young.

6.   friend?   ▷
     happy/sad?
     happy.

7.   teacher?   ▷
     short/tall?
     tall.

8.   Ask your own question.   ▷

STUDY 1

Forms of the verb **be** (**am**, **are**, **is**): *My mother is tall, too.*

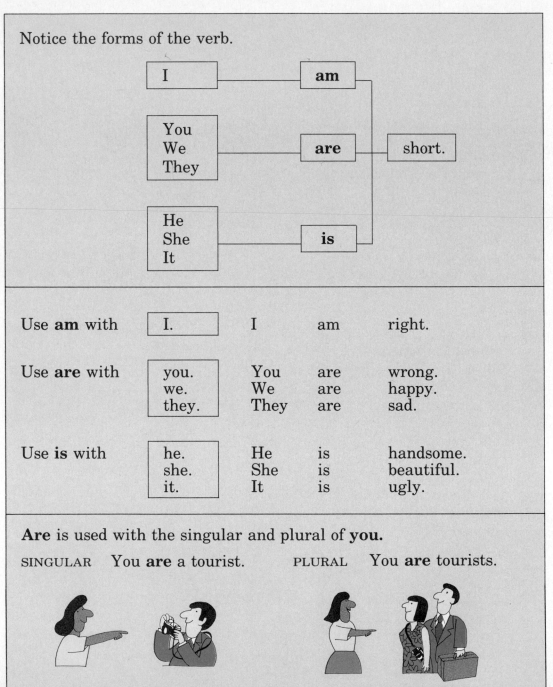

Notice the forms of the verb.

I	**am**
You We They	**are** short.
He She It	**is**

Use **am** with   I.   I am right.

Use **are** with
you.   You are wrong.
we.   We are happy.
they.   They are sad.

Use **is** with
he.   He is handsome.
she.   She is beautiful.
it.   It is ugly.

Are is used with the singular and plural of **you.**

SINGULAR   You **are** a tourist.   PLURAL   You **are** tourists.

PRACTICE

A. Complete the sentences about Bill and Linda. Use the correct form of the verb *be*.

EX.   Linda **is** a tourist.
      Linda and Bill **are** in the United States.

1. China _is_ beautiful.
2. Linda _is_ Chinese.
3. England _is_ beautiful.
4. Bill _is_ English.
5. Bill _is_ handsome.
6. Bill and Linda _are_ friends.
7. They _are_ happy.

Linda   Bill

B. Complete the sentences about you and your classmates. Use the correct form of the verb *be*.

1. We _are_ in class.
2. I _am_ present.
3. My classmates _are_ present, too.
4. We _are_ friends.
5. You _are_ right.
6. I _am_ wrong.

STUDY 2

Contractions of the verb **be** (**'m, 's, 're**): *He's tall and I'm short.*

Notice the contracted forms of the verb **be**.

SINGULAR

| I am
I'm | short. |

| You are
You're | short. |

| He is
He's | tall. |

| She is
She's | tall. |

| It is
It's | high. |

PLURAL

| We are
We're | happy. |

| You are
You're | sad. |

| They are
They're | sick. |

Use the contractions in conversation.

PRACTICE

A. Look at the pictures and answer the questions.

EX. Are you American?
⇨ **No. I'm English.**

Is he Colombian?
⇨ **Yes. He's Colombian.**

1. Are they absent?
⇨ No. They're present.

2. Are we in California?
⇨ Yes. We're.

3. Is she sad?
⇨ No. She's Happy.

4. Am I sick?
⇨ Yes. you're.

5. Are you tourists?
⇨ No. We're a doctor.

6. Ask your own question.
⇨

B. Look at the map. Ask and answer questions.

EX. Is Manila in Japan?
    No. It's in the Philippines.*

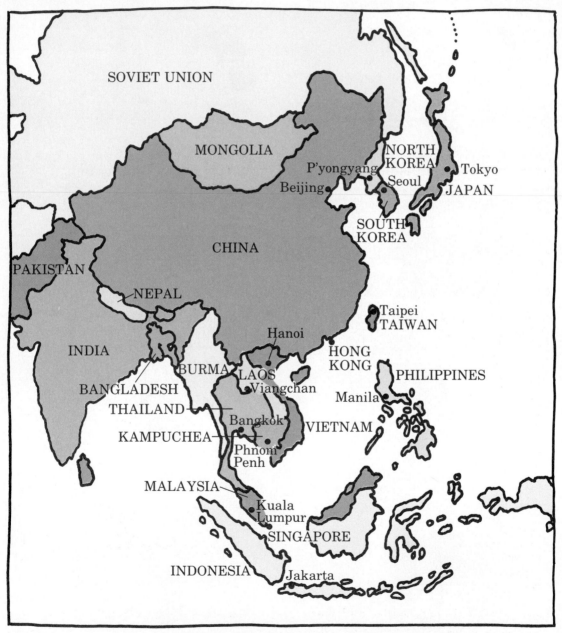

*NOTE: Use **the** with three of the countries on this map: the Philippines, the People's Republic of China, the Soviet Union.

C. Look at the pictures and answer the questions.

EX. Is this Vanh?
▷ **No. It's Lynn.**

Lynn

Is this a man?
▷ **Yes. It's a man.**

1. Is this Toshi?
▷ Yes. It's Toshi.

Toshi

2. Is this a saleswoman?
▷ NO. It's a doctor.

3. Is this Portugal?
▷ No. It's Puerto Rico.

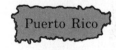
Puerto Rico

4. Is this a woman?
▷ Yes. It's a woman.

5. Is this a dog?
▷ Yes. It's a dog.

6. Ask your own questions.
Ask about your classmates
and about the maps in your
classroom.
▷

STUDY 3

Plurals of nouns: *We're brothers.*

Notice the formation of plurals with different nouns.

I'm	a lawyer.	We're	lawyers.
You're	a mechanic.	You're	mechanics.
He's	a cook.	They're	cooks.
She's	a nurse.	They're	nurses.
It's	a city.	They're	cities.
It's	a watch.	They're	watches.

San Francisco

Los Angeles

Omit the article **a** in the plural.

PRACTICE

Make sentences like the models. Use the cues.

EX. He/doctor.
They.

⟡ He's a doctor.
Really? They're doctors, too.

I/tourist.
We.

⟡ I'm a tourist.
Really? We're tourists, too.

1. I/student.
We.

⟡ I'm a student
Really?. we're students, too.

2. She/nurse.
They.

⟡ She's a nurse
They're nurses, too.

3. He/teacher.
They.

⟡ He's a teacher
They're a teacher, too.

4. I/scientist.
We.

⟡ I'm a scientist.
We're a scientists, too.

5. I/lawyer.
We.

⟡ I'm a lawyer
We're a lawyes, too.

6. She/mechanic.
They.

⟡ She's a mechanic
They're a mechanics, too.

7. Make your own
sentences.

⟡

STUDY 4

Yes-no questions with the verb **be:** *Are you and Jim friends?*

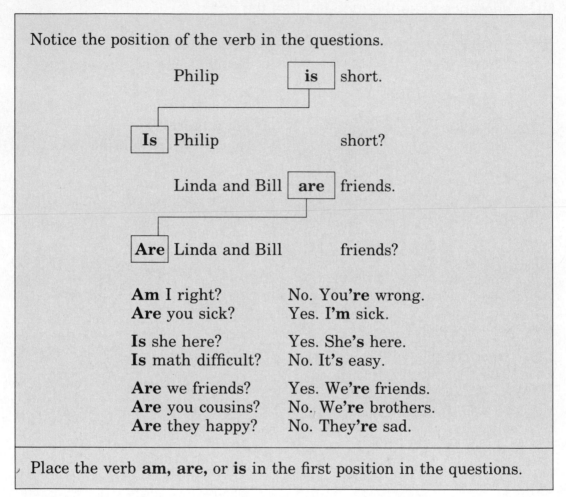

Notice the position of the verb in the questions.

Philip   **is**   short.

Is   Philip   short?

Linda and Bill   **are**   friends.

Are   Linda and Bill   friends?

Am I right?	No. You**'re** wrong.
Are you sick?	Yes. I**'m** sick.
Is she here?	Yes. She**'s** here.
Is math difficult?	No. It**'s** easy.
Are we friends?	Yes. We**'re** friends.
Are you cousins?	No. We**'re** brothers.
Are they happy?	No. They**'re** sad.

Place the verb **am, are,** or **is** in the first position in the questions.

 PRACTICE

Look at the pictures. Ask and answer the questions using the cues.

EX.   Linda/tourist?
▷   **Is Linda a tourist?**
     Yes. She's a tourist.

you/sick?
⇨ **Are you sick?**
No. I'm fine.

1. Debbie/nurse?
⇨ Is Debbie a nurse?
Yes. She's a nurse.

2. Aki and Julia/students?
⇨ Are Aki and Julia students?
No. They're a doctors.

3. Linda and Toshi/tourists?
⇨ Are Linda and Toshi tourists?
Yes. They're tourists.

Japan

4. Yoko/Chinese?
⇨ Is Yoko chinese?
No. She's Japanese

2 + 2 = 4

5. Robert/right?
⇨ Is Robert right?
Yes. He's right.

6. I/tall?
⇨ I'm tall?
Yes. You're tall.

7. Ask about your classmates.
⇨

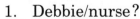

LISTEN

A. Look at the pictures below. Then listen to each sentence and write the letter of the sentence next to the matching picture.

1. _____   2. _____

3. _____   4. _____

5. _____   6. _____

B. Listen to each question. Then choose the correct answer.

1. a. Yes. She's in China.
    b. Yes. It's in China.
    c. Yes. He's in China.

2. a. No. They're friends.
    b. Yes. He's a friend.
    c. Yes. You're cousins.

3. a. Yes. We're in Caracas.
    b. Yes. You're in Caracas.
    c. Yes. I'm in class.

4. a. Yes. She's in Puerto Rico.
    b. Yes. It's in Puerto Rico.
    c. Yes. He's in Puerto Rico.

5. a. No. It's in Mexico.
    b. Yes. She's in the U.S.
    c. No. She's in the U.S.

6. a. Yes. I'm short.
    b. Yes. You're tall.
    c. No. I'm short.

SPEAK

A. Listen to the conversation.

PHILIP: Hello, Carlos. Hi, Aki.
CARLOS: Hi, Philip.
AKI: Hi, Philip.
LINDA: Are you and Aki students?
PHILIP: I'm a student. Aki's a doctor.
AKI: What about you, Linda?
LINDA: I'm a tourist.

B. Practice the conversation with three classmates. Use your own information.

STUDENT 1: Hello, _Steves_. Hi, _ElizobetH_.
STUDENT 2: Hi, _Mary_.
STUDENT 3: Hi, _steve_.
STUDENT 4: Are you and _Steves_ students?
STUDENT 1: I'm a _Student_. _He is a proffesor_
STUDENT 3: What about you, _Mary_?
STUDENT 4: I'm a _Teacher_.

C. Now close your book and practice the conversation with three different classmates.

READ

A. Read the letter. Then answer the questions.

Dear Ricardo,

    This is my family. We are in New York now. My father is a doctor. He's Colombian. He's tall. My mother is a nurse. She's Venezuelan. She's short. My mother and father are old.

    My sisters are young. They're students. My brother and I are young. We're students, too. My brother is tall. My sisters are short.

    We're happy in the United States.

    Write soon.

1. Is the family in Colombia or New York?
2. Is the mother a doctor or a nurse?
3. Is the brother short?
4. Is the family happy or sad in the United States?
5. Are the sisters students?

B. Ask your own questions about the family.

THINK

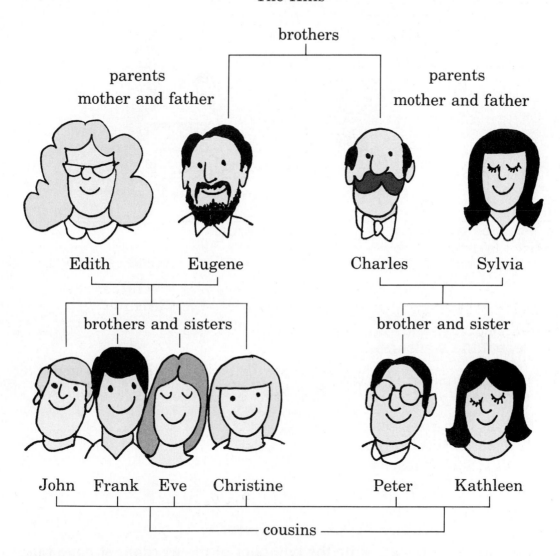

The Hills

brothers

parents
mother and father

parents
mother and father

Edith   Eugene

Charles   Sylvia

brothers and sisters

brother and sister

John   Frank   Eve   Christine

Peter   Kathleen

cousins

Look at the family tree and ask questions.

1. Are Eugene and Charles brothers or cousins?
2. Are Peter and Kathleen brother and sister?
3. Are Sylvia and Charles parents?

Ask your own questions.

PRONOUNCE: [iy]

sheep	high front close, tense
	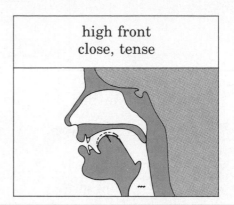

A. Practice the sound [iy]. Repeat the words.

he	she	Eve
Edith	Peter	teacher
Eugene	Kathleen	Christine

B. Repeat the sentences.

1. Christine, this is Peter.
2. Is Peter a teacher?
3. Yes. He's a teacher.
4. Is Eve a teacher?
5. Yes. She's a teacher.
6. Is this a sheep?
7. Yes. It's a sheep.

C. On a sheet of paper, write the numbers of the words that have the sound [iy].

1. we	6. are	11. Peter	16. sister
2. she	7. Eve	12. Bill	17. friend
3. I	8. is	13. Kathleen	18. English
4. he	9. Christine	14. Linda	19. teacher
5. it	10. this	15. Edith	20. sheep

CONVERSATION

Identifying a Person

JACK: Excuse me.

Are you Carolyn Jackson?

BARBARA: No, I'm not. I'm Barbara Stern.

JACK: Is Carolyn here today?

BARBARA: No, she's not. She's sick.

Are you a teacher here, too?

JACK: Yes, I am.

BARBARA: What's your name?

JACK: Oh, my name is Jack Newman.

BARBARA: It's nice to meet you, Jack.

33

INTERACTION

A. Make sentences like the models. Use the cues.

EX. you Carolyn Jackson?
Barbara Stern.
Carolyn here today?
sick.

▷ **Excuse me. Are you Carolyn Jackson?**
No, I'm not. I'm Barbara Stern.
Is Carolyn here today?
No, she's not. She's sick.

1. he Philip Sullivan?
Jack Newman.
he English?
American.

▷ Excuse me. Is he Philip Sullivan?
No. he's not.

2. you a tourist?
a saleswoman.
you French?
Italian.

▷ Excuse me, Are you a tourist.

3. she American?
Australian.
she sick?
fine.

▷

4. Ask your own questions.

▷

B. Make sentences like the models. Use the cues.

EX. you a teacher here?
Yes.

▷ **Are you a teacher here?**
Yes, I am.

1. you a tourist here?
Yes.

▷ Are you a tourist here?
Yes, I am.

2. you Australian?
   Yes.

   ▷ *Are you Australian?*
   Yes. I am

3. you happy here?
   Yes.

   ▷ *Are you happy here?*
   Yes. I am.

4. you a mechanic in
   Australia?
   Yes.

   ▷ *Are you a mechanic in*
   Australia?
   Yes. I am

5. you happy in Australia,
   too?
   Yes.

   ▷ *Are you happy in Australia too?*
   Yes. I am happy in Australia
   too.

6. Ask a classmate a question.   ▷

C. Make sentences like the models. Use the cues.

EX. your name?
Jack Newman.

▷ **What's your name?**
My name's Jack Newman.
It's nice to meet you.

1. your name?
   Barbara Stern.

   ▷ *What's your name?*
   My name's Barbara Stern.
   It's nice to meet you.

2. your name?
   Carolyn Jackson.

   ▷ *What's your name?*
   My name's Carolyn Jackson.
   It's nice to meet you.

3. your name?
   Philip Sullivan.

   ▷ *What's your name?*
   My name's Philip Sullivan.
   It's nice to meet you.

4. Ask a classmate what his
   or her name is.

   What's your name?
   ▷ *My name's Elizabeth Morrison*
   It's nice to meet you.

STUDY 1

Affirmative short answers with **be:** *Yes, I am.*

Notice the omission of the noun or adjective in the short answers.

Are you hungry?	**Yes, I am.**
Am I friendly?	**Yes, you are.**
Is Bill a salesman?	**Yes, he is.**
Is Linda sick?	**Yes, she is.**
Is London nice?	**Yes, it is.**
Are you and Linda thirsty?	**Yes, we are.**
Are Paul and I handsome?	**Yes, you are.**
Are Philip and Vanh friends?	**Yes, they are.**

No contractions are used in short answers beginning with **Yes.**

PRACTICE

A. Answer with affirmative short answers. Use *he, she, it,* and *they*.

EX. Is Barbara friendly?
▷ **Yes, she is.**

Jack   Barbara

Are Barbara and Jack
happy?
▷ **Yes, they are.**

1. Is Barbara hungry?
▷ Yes, she is.

2. Is Jack thirsty?
▷ yes, he is

Jack   Barbara

3. Is math difficult?

▷ yes, it is.

Philip

4. Is Philip unhappy?

▷ Yes, he is.

5. Are Jim and Carolyn tall?

▷ yes, they are

6. Is Carolyn happy?

▷ yes, she is

Jim   Carolyn

7. Is San Francisco in the United States?

▷ yes, it is.

San Francisco

8. Is it beautiful?

▷ yes, it is

B. Ask yes-no questions using the cues. Answer with affirmative short answers using *I,* *you,* **and** *we.*

EX.   you/hungry?
 ⇨ **Are you hungry?**
    Yes, I am.

1. you and Jack/friends?
 ⇨ Are you and Jack Friends?
    Yes, we are.

2. you/thirsty?
 ⇨ Are you thirsty?
    Yes. I am.

3. you/tourists?
 ⇨ Are you a tourists?
    Yes, we are.

4. you/doctors?
 ⇨ Are you or doctors?
    yes, we are.

5. I/friendly?
 ⇨ Am I friendly?
    Yes, you are.

39

6. you and I/happy?
➤ Are you and I happy?
Yes, we are.

7. you and Philip/students?
➤ Are you and Philip a students?
Yes, we are.

8. I/tall?
➤ Am I tall?
Yes, you are

9. you/a salesman?
➤ Are you a salesman?
Yes, I am

10. I/handsome?
➤ Am I handsome?
Yes you are.

11. Ask a question about
    yourself.
➤

STUDY 2

Negative statements with **be**: *I'm not Carolyn Jackson.*

Notice the position of **not**.

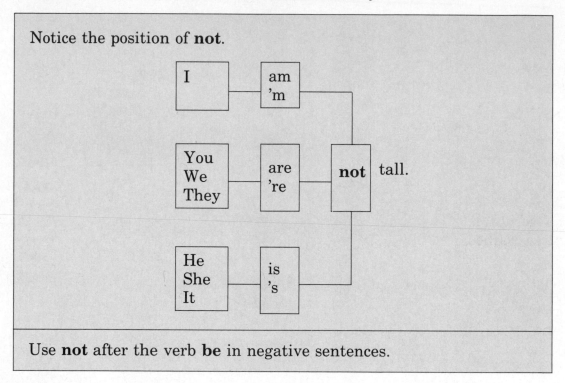

Use **not** after the verb **be** in negative sentences.

 PRACTICE

Look at the pictures and answer the questions. Answer with affirmative or negative statements.

EX. Are you from Tokyo?
▷ **Yes. I'm from Tokyo.**

Is Tokyo in China?
▷ **No. It's not in China.**

Are you and Linda students?
▷ **No. We're not students.**

Tokyo

1. Am I short?
   ▷

2. Is Ramón in Costa Rica?
   ▷

   Mexico

3. Is Mary sick?
   ▷

4. Are Philip and Carlos at school?
   ▷

5. Are you Carolyn Jackson?
   ▷

   Barbara Stern

6. Are Jack and I cooks?
   ▷

7. Is Japan a city?
   ▷

   Japan

8. Ask your own question.
   ▷

STUDY 3

Negative short answers with **be**: *No, I'm not.*

Notice the position of **not**.

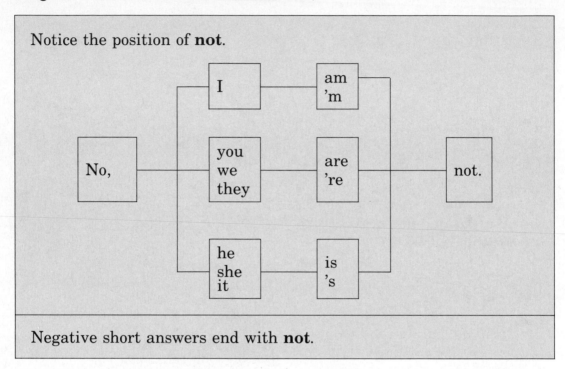

Negative short answers end with **not**.

 # PRACTICE

A. Answer the questions with negative short answers.

EX. Is New York in England?
  ▷ **No, it's not.**

1. Is Jack in London?
  ▷

2. Are Jack and Helen
    cousins?
  ▷

3. Are you and Helen friends?
  ▷

4. Is English difficult?
  ▷

5. Am I absent today?
  ▷

6. Are you sick today?
  ▷

7. Is Helen from Japan?
  ▷

B. Look at the map. Ask yes-no questions and answer with short answers.

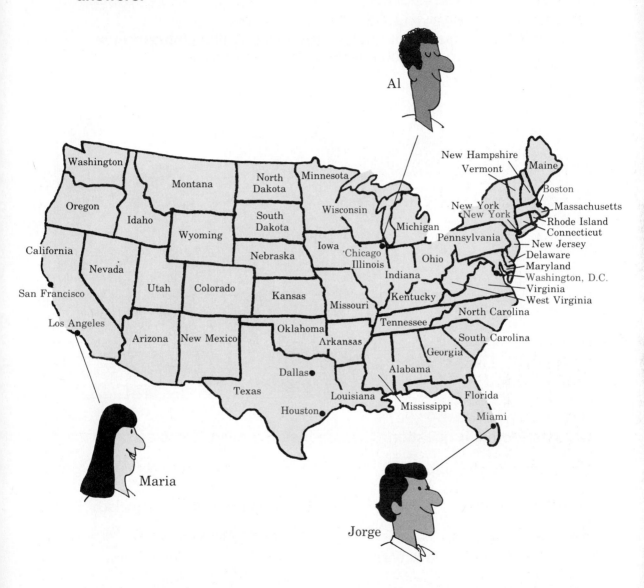

EX. Is Chicago in California?
⇨ **No, it's not.**

Is Maria in California?
⇨ **Yes, she is.**

Are Jorge and Al in New York?
⇨ **No, they're not.**

Is San Francisco in California?
⇨ **Yes, it is.**

LISTEN

A. Listen to the questions and answers about the picture below. Write the answer to each question after you hear it.

1. _____

2. _____

3. _____

4. _____

5. _____

6. _____

B. Listen to each question. Then choose the correct answer.

1. a. No. They're Japanese.
    b. Yes, they are.
    c. Yes, she is.

2. a. Yes, they are.
    b. No. She's in New York.
    c. Yes, he is.

3. a. No. She's fine.
    b. Yes. She's present.
    c. Yes, he is.

4. a. No. She's sick.
    b. No. She's my friend.
    c. No, he's not.

5. a. Yes, she is.
    b. She's Brazilian.
    c. She's in San Francisco.

6. a. No. He's sick.
    b. No. He's Colombian.
    c. Yes. He's fine.

7. a. Yes, it is.
    b. No, it isn't.
    c. Yes, they are.

8. a. No. It's in Japan.
    b. No, they aren't.
    c. Yes, it is.

SPEAK

A. Listen to the conversation.

NICK:	Excuse me, are you a student here?
LYNN:	Yes, I am. I'm Lynn Reed. What's your name?
NICK:	My name's Nick Kouros. I'm a student, too.
LYNN:	Nice to meet you, Nick.
NICK:	Nice to meet you, too.
LYNN:	Are you from Rome?
NICK:	No, I'm not. I'm from Athens.
LYNN:	Really? Is Athens nice?
NICK:	Yes. It's beautiful.

B. Practice the conversation with a classmate.
Use your own information.

STUDENT 1:	Excuse me, are you a student here?
STUDENT 2:	Yes, I am. I'm _____. What's your name?
STUDENT 1:	My name's _____. I'm a student, too.
STUDENT 2:	Nice to meet you, _____.
STUDENT 1:	Nice to meet you, too.
STUDENT 2:	Are you from _____?
STUDENT 1:	No, I'm not. I'm from _____.
STUDENT 2:	Really? Is _____ nice?
STUDENT 1:	Yes. It's beautiful.

C. Now close your book and practice the conversation with a different classmate.

READ

A. Read the story and answer the questions.

Tourists In Europe

Europe is big and it is interesting. Margaret Vitali is in Europe. She is a tourist. She is in Madrid. Madrid is not a country. Madrid is a city in Spain. Spain is beautiful.

Michael and Carol White are brother and sister. They are in Europe, too. They are in Paris. Paris is a city in France.

Michael and Carol are tourists from Chicago. Michael is a pilot. Carol is a teacher. They are happy in Paris.

1. Is Europe big?
2. Is it interesting?
3. Is Margaret a tourist?
4. Is she in the United States?
5. Is Margaret in Madrid?
6. Are Madrid and Paris cities?
7. Are Michael and Carol in France?
8. Is Paris a city?
9. Is France a city?
10. Is Michael a teacher?

B. Now ask questions about Michael and Carol White.

THINK

Ask questions about the pictures.

1.

EX.   Is Joseph Vitali hungry?
  ⇨   **Yes, he is.**

2.

3.

PRONOUNCE: [i], [iy]

ship [i]

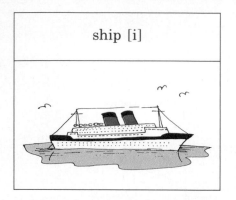

sheep [iy]

A. Repeat the words and contrast [i] and [iy].

| ship | sick | this | sister | it | is |
| sheep | she | he | Greek | Eve | teacher |

B. Repeat the sentences.

1. Is this Peter?
2. No. It's Nick.
3. Is Nick English?
4. No. He's Greek.

5. Is Bill a teacher?
6. No, he's not.
7. Is he sick?
8. Yes, he is.

C. On a sheet of paper, write the numbers of the words that have the sound [i]. Then listen to the words again, and write the numbers of the words that have the sound [iy].

1. we	5. teacher	9. ship	13. is	17. she
2. I	6. English	10. friend	14. Eve	18. sick
3. it	7. Greek	11. Peter	15. Linda	19. nurse
4. are	8. Nick	12. he	16. sister	20. this

CONVERSATION

Greeting a Friend

MRS. NEWMAN: Good morning.

ALICE: Hello, Mrs. Newman.

How are you?

MRS. NEWMAN: I'm fine, thank you.

And you?

ALICE: I'm fine, thanks.

Where's Mr. Newman?

MRS. NEWMAN: He's home.

ALICE: How is he?

MRS. NEWMAN: He's sick. He's in bed.

ALICE: Oh, that's too bad.

INTERACTION

A. Look at the pictures and make sentences like the models.

EX. Bill?
▷ **Where's Bill?**
He's in bed.

1. Linda?
▷

New York

2. Oscar?
▷

3. Ramón?
▷

Mexico

4. Toshi?
▷

San Francisco

5. Lynn?
▷

B. Look at the pictures and make sentences like the models.

EX. How's Mr. Newman?
  ⇨ **He's sick. He's in bed.
  Oh, that's too bad.**

  How are Michael and
  Carol?
  ⇨ **They're fine. They're in
  Paris.
  Oh, that's wonderful.**

1. How's Vanh?
  ⇨

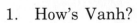

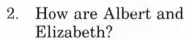

2. How are Albert and
  Elizabeth?
  ⇨

3. How's Margaret?
  ⇨

Madrid

4. How's Linda?
  ⇨

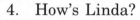

United States

STUDY 1

Information questions with **be**: *How is he?*

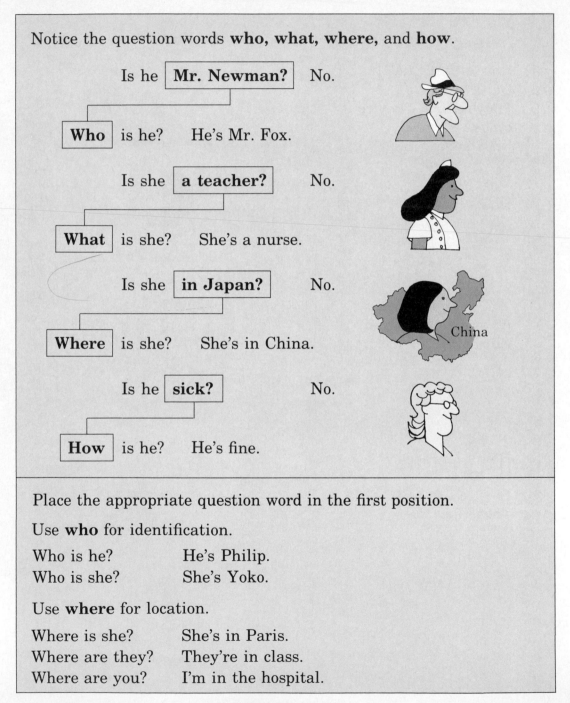

Notice the question words **who, what, where,** and **how**.

Is he | **Mr. Newman?** | No.

Who is he?   He's Mr. Fox.

Is she | **a teacher?** | No.

What is she?   She's a nurse.

Is she | **in Japan?** | No.

Where is she?   She's in China.

China

Is he | **sick?** | No.

How is he?   He's fine.

Place the appropriate question word in the first position.

Use **who** for identification.

Who is he?   He's Philip.
Who is she?   She's Yoko.

Use **where** for location.

Where is she?   She's in Paris.
Where are they?   They're in class.
Where are you?   I'm in the hospital.

Use **what** for classification.

What is it?	It's a dog.
What are they?	They're cameras.

Use **how** for quality or state.

How are you?	I'm fine.
How is he?	He's sick.

PRACTICE

A. Ask information questions with *what*, *where*, or *how*. Look at the pictures and answer the questions.

EX. Is Mr. Collins a doctor?
No, he's not.
▷ **What is he?**
He's a lawyer.

lawyer

Are they sick?
No, they're not.
▷ **How are they?**
They're fine.

Are you in California?
No, we're not.
▷ **Where are you?**
We're in Texas.

Texas

1. Is Donald home?
   No, he's not.

   ⇨

2. Is Chicago a country?
   No, it's not.
   ⇨

   Chicago

3. Are you sick?
   No, I'm not.
   ⇨

4. Is Lisbon in Spain?
   No, it's not.
   ⇨

   Portugal   Spain
   Lisbon

5. Is Bill well?
   No, he's not.
   ⇨

6. Are Korea and Thailand
   cities?
   No, they're not.
   ⇨

   Korea   Thailand

B. Look at the answers. Then ask appropriate questions with *what*, *where*, or *how*.

EX. <u>**Where are John and Mary**</u> ?
John and Mary are in Berlin.

<u>**How are you**</u> ?
I'm sick.

1. _____?
He's a lawyer.

2. _____?
I'm fine.

3. _____?
Sylvia and Edith are in New York.

4. _____?
We're fine.

5. _____?
Paul Collins is in Caracas.

6. _____?
San Francisco is a city.

7. _____?
Lima is in Peru.

8. Ask your own question.

STUDY 2

The articles **a** and **the**: *The man is tall.*

Notice the use of **a** and **the**.

This is **a book**.

The book is small.

A boy and **a man** are
waiting for a bus.

The boy is short.
The man is tall.

The moon is in **the sky**.

Use **a** when you first mention something.
Use **the** to be more specific, to refer to something again, or to talk
about something unique.

 ## PRACTICE

A. Look at the pictures and answer the questions.

EX. What is she?
 ▷ **She's a doctor.**

What is this?
 ▷ **It's a hospital.**

1. What is this?
   ⇨

2. What is he?
   ⇨

3. What is she?
   ⇨

4. What is this?
   ⇨

5. What is she?
   ⇨

6. What is he?
   ⇨

7. What is this?
   ⇨

8. What is she?
   ⇨

B. Make sentences about each picture. Use the article *the*.

EX. A woman and a man are in
class.
⇨ **The woman is a teacher.**
The man is a student.

A pilot and a teacher are in Paris.
⇨ **The pilot is tall.**
The teacher is short.

1. A brother and a sister are
in Europe.

⇨

2. A man and a woman are in
this office.

⇨

3. We are in a city and in a
country.

⇨

Caracas

Venezuela

4. A boy and a girl are on a
bus.

⇨

5. A man and a woman are friends.
⇨

STUDY 3

The articles **a** and **an**: *It's a book. It's an apple.*

Notice the sound after **a** and **an**.

It's **a** book.

It's **an** eraser.

It's **a** pencil.

It's **an** apple.

Use **a** before consonant sounds.
Use **an** before vowel sounds.

PRACTICE

Ask and answer a question for each picture.

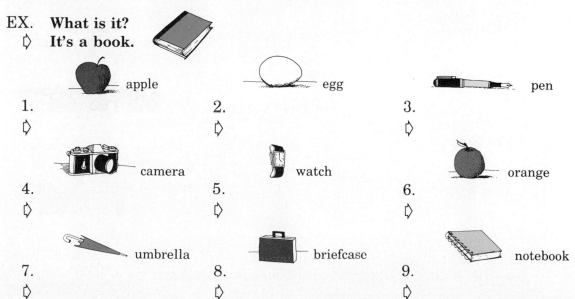

EX. **What is it?**
  ▷ **It's a book.**

　　apple　　　　　　　　egg　　　　　　　　pen

1.　　　　　　　　2.　　　　　　　　3.
▷　　　　　　　　▷　　　　　　　　▷

　　camera　　　　　　watch　　　　　　orange

4.　　　　　　　　5.　　　　　　　　6.
▷　　　　　　　　▷　　　　　　　　▷

　　umbrella　　　　　briefcase　　　　　notebook

7.　　　　　　　　8.　　　　　　　　9.
▷　　　　　　　　▷　　　　　　　　▷

STUDY 4

Articles with singular and plural nouns:
He's a pilot. The boys are students.

Notice the articles **a** and **an** with singular and plural nouns.

He's **a tourist**.

They're **tourists**.

It's **an apple**.

They're **apples**.

Notice the article **the** with singular and plural nouns.

The student is intelligent.

The students are intelligent.

The apple is good.

The apples are good.

Use **a** and **an** with singular nouns only.
Use **the** with singular and plural nouns.

PRACTICE

Make plural sentences.

EX. He's a lawyer.
 ▷ **They're lawyers.**

 I'm happy.
 ▷ **We're happy.**

 The lawyer is intelligent.
 ▷ **The lawyers are intelligent.**

1. It's a school.
 ▷ *They're schools.*

2. The class is big.
 ▷ *The classes are big.*

3. I'm a nurse.
 ▷ *We are nurses.*

4. The student is tall.
 ▷ *The students are tall.*

5. It's an umbrella.
 ▷ *They are umbrellas.*

6. She's a friend.
 ▷ *They are friend.*

7. The hospital is big.
 ▷

8. You're a student.
 ▷

9. He's a travel agent.
 ▷

STUDY 5

Modifiers of nouns: *He's a good doctor.*

Notice the position of the modifiers **good, nice, art,** and **night**.

The doctor is good.	He's a	**good**	doctor.
The watches are nice.	They're	**nice**	watches.
The book is on art.	It's an	**art**	book.
The classes are at night.	They're	**night**	classes.

Modifiers come before the nouns they modify.

 # PRACTICE

A. Answer the questions with *yes*. Make sentences with modified nouns.

EX.   Is the story interesting?
   ▷   **Yes. It's an interesting story.**

1.   Are the problems easy?
   ▷   *Yes. they are easy Problems.*

2.   Is the city big?
   ▷

3.   Is the country beautiful?
   ▷   *Yes. It is a*

4.   Is the briefcase big?
   ▷   *Yes. It is a big briefcase*

5.   Is the map old?
   ▷   *Yes. It is a old map.*

B. Complete the sentences. Put the modifier before the noun.

EX.   A book on art is **an art book**.
   A class in English is **an English class**.
   An article in a newspaper is **a newspaper article**.

1. A teacher of chemistry is ⎯⎯ a chemist ⎯⎯ .
2. A book on science is ⎯ a science book ⎯
3. A teacher of geography is ⎯ a geography teacher ⎯
4. A class in math is ⎯ a math class ⎯
5. A book on history is ⎯ a history book ⎯
6. A lesson in English is ⎯ an English lesson. ⎯
7. A bed in a hospital is ⎯ a hospital bed ⎯
8. An exercise on grammar is ⎯ a grammar exercise. ⎯

C. Now ask and answer a question for each picture.

EX.   ◊ **What is it?**
     It's an English book.

◊ **What is he?**
He's a math teacher.

1. ◊

2. ◊

3. ◊

4. ◊

LISTEN

A. Listen and write the questions and answers.

1. _____?

   _____.

2. _____?

   _____.

3. _____?

   _____.

4. _____?

   _____.

B. Listen to each question. Then choose the correct answer.

1. a. Bogotá is big.
   b. It's in Colombia.
   c. It's a city.

2. a. It's a city.
   b. It's interesting.
   c. It's in the United States.

3. a. It's in the United States.
   b. It's in England.
   c. It's beautiful.

4. a. Yes. It's in Italy.
   b. It's in China.
   c. Yes, it is.

5. a. They're fine, too.
   b. They're old, too.
   c. They're cities, too.

6. a. He's a teacher.
   b. He's sick.
   c. He's in the United States.

SPEAK

A. Listen to the conversation.

MR. TANAKA:	Good evening, Miss Jackson.
MISS JACKSON:	Hello, Mr. Tanaka. How are you?
MR. TANAKA:	I'm fine, thank you. And you?
MISS JACKSON:	Fine, thanks.
	Where's Mrs. Tanaka?
MR. TANAKA:	She's home. She's sick.
MISS JACKSON:	Oh, that's too bad.

B. Practice the conversation with a classmate. Use your own names, the names of relatives, and the words that follow the dialogue.

STUDENT 1:	_____1_____, _____.
STUDENT 2:	Hello, _____. How are you?
STUDENT 1:	I'm _____2_____, thank you. And you?
STUDENT 2:	_____2_____, thanks.
	Where's _____?
STUDENT 1:	She's (He's) home. She's (He's) sick.
STUDENT 2:	Oh, that's too bad.

1.	2.
Good morning	very well
Good afternoon	fine
Good evening	

C. Now close your book and practice the conversation with a different classmate.

READ

An Interview with *Eugene and Edith Hill*
—*Susan Blake*

SUSAN BLAKE: Good evening, Mr. and Mrs. Hill. How are you?

MR. HILL: We're fine, thank you.

SUSAN BLAKE: Are you from New York, Mr. Hill?

MR. HILL: No, Susan. I'm from Boston.

SUSAN BLAKE: What about you, Mrs. Hill?

MRS. HILL: Yes. I'm from New York.

SUSAN BLAKE: Please tell me about your job, Mr. Hill.

MR. HILL: Well, I'm a computer programmer in this office.

SUSAN BLAKE: Really? That's wonderful. Are you a computer programmer too, Mrs. Hill?

MRS. HILL: No. I'm an engineer.

SUSAN BLAKE: That's very interesting. Thank you, Mr. and Mrs. Hill.

MRS. HILL: You're welcome, Susan.

Match the sentences.

1. How are you?
2. Are you from New York?
3. Please tell me about your job.
4. Are you a computer programmer, too?
5. Thank you, Mr. and Mrs. Hill.

a. I'm a computer programmer.
b. We're fine.
c. No. I'm from Boston.
d. You're welcome.
e. No. I'm an engineer.

THINK

Play *20 Questions* with a group or with the class.

1. **STUDENT 1: What is it?**

STUDENT 2:	Is it big?
STUDENT 1:	No, it's not.
STUDENT 3:	Is it a book?
STUDENT 1:	No, it's not.
STUDENT 4:	Is it a camera?
STUDENT 1:	Yes, it is.

2. **STUDENT 1: Where is it?**

STUDENT 2:	Is it in Europe?
STUDENT 1:	Yes, it is.
STUDENT 3:	Is it in Greece?
STUDENT 1:	No, it's not.
STUDENT 4:	Is it in England?
STUDENT 1:	Yes, it is.
STUDENT 5:	Is it the capital?
STUDENT 1:	Yes, it is.
STUDENT 6:	Is it London?
STUDENT 1:	Yes, it is.

3. **STUDENT 1: Who is it?**

STUDENT 2:	Is it a man?
STUDENT 1:	Yes, it is.
STUDENT 3:	Is he intelligent?
STUDENT 1:	Yes, he is.
STUDENT 4:	Is he a doctor?
STUDENT 1:	No, he's not.
STUDENT 5:	Is he a teacher?
STUDENT 1:	Yes, he is.
STUDENT 6:	Is he Oscar?
STUDENT 1:	Yes, he is.

PRONOUNCE: [z]

zip	voiced, alveolar
	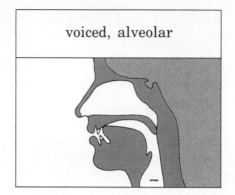

A. Repeat the words.

is	doctors	Rose	memorize	busy
please	he's	nurses	easy	zip

B. Repeat the sentences.

1. Is James in Brazil?
   No. He's in Lisbon.
2. Please tell Elizabeth.
   Rose is busy.
3. Are Charles and Rose doctors?
   No. They're nurses.

C. On a sheet of paper, write the numbers of the words that have the sound [z].

1. please
2. is
3. student
4. memorize
5. doctors

6. Rose
7. easy
8. teachers
9. class
10. he's

CONVERSATION

Calling a Friend

MRS. JACKSON: Hello?

BARBARA: Hello, Mrs. Jackson.

This is Barbara.

Is Carolyn there?

MRS. JACKSON: Yes, she is.

Just a minute, Barbara.

CAROLYN: Hi, Barbara.

BARBARA: Hi. What are you doing?

CAROLYN: I'm packing.

BARBARA: Oh? Where are you going?

CAROLYN: I'm going to Boston.

69

INTERACTION

A. Ask and answer questions like the models. Use the cues.

EX. you?
packing.
⇨ **What are you doing?**
I'm packing.

1. I?
writing.
⇨

2. he?
singing.
⇨

3. they?
watching television (TV).
⇨

4. she?
talking.
⇨

5. Ask your own question.
⇨

B. Ask and answer questions. Use the cues.

EX. you/going?
to Boston.
 Where are you going?
I'm going to Boston.

1. Philip/studying?
in the library.

2. he/eating?
in the kitchen.

3. they/working?
in the office.

4. they/talking?
at school.

5. Ask your own question.

74

B. Look at the pictures and answer the questions.

EX.   What are you doing,
      listening or talking?
    ▷ **I'm listening.**

1. What is Helen doing,
   sleeping or working?
   ▷

2. What is Mr. Collins doing,
   laughing or crying?
   ▷

3. What is Barbara doing,
   reading or writing?
   ▷

4. What is he writing,
   a letter or a story?
   ▷

5. What are they reading,
   a book or a newspaper?
   ▷

6. What are they doing,
   singing or playing the
   guitar?

   ▷

7. What am I playing,
   the guitar or the piano?

   ▷

8. What is Linda doing,
   eating or drinking?

   ▷

9. What are they doing,
   listening or singing?

   ▷

10. What's the teacher doing,
    teaching or studying?

    ▷

11. Ask your classmate a
    question.

    ▷

STUDY 2

Negative statements in the present progressive: *I'm not eating.*

Notice the placement of **not**.

I'm	**not**	sleeping.
He's	**not**	singing.
You're	**not**	working.

Place **not** after the verb **be (am, are, is)**.

 ## PRACTICE

Describe the pictures using the cues.

EX. I/work
⇨ **I'm not working.**
I'm drinking coffee.

She/write
⇨ **She's not writing.**
She's reading.

1. We/laugh
⇨

2. It/eat
⇨

3. He/play the guitar
⇩

4. They/dance
⇩

5. I/listen to the radio
⇩

6. You/work
⇩

7. She/drink coffee
⇩

8. What about you?
⇩

STUDY 3

Yes-no questions in the present progressive:
Is she going to Boston?

Notice the word order in the questions.

> You | **are** | eating an apple.
>
> **Are** you eating an apple?
>
> **Is** she eating an orange?
> **Am** I eating an orange?

For questions in the present progressive, use the word order for questions with the verb **be (am, are, is)**. (See page 26.)

 # PRACTICE

Look at the answers. Then ask appropriate yes-no questions.

EX. **Am I singing well**?
No. You're not singing well.

Is she asking a question?
Yes. She's asking a question.

1. _____?
Yes. He's reading an art book.

2. _____?
   No. The students are not
   dancing.

3. _____?
   Yes. We're going now.

4. _____?
   Yes. They're listening to the
   radio.

5. _____?
   No. She's not working today.

6. _____?
   Yes. He's sleeping now.

7. _____?
   Yes. I'm crying.

STUDY 4

Short answers in the present progressive: *Yes, she is.*

Notice the short answers.

Are you Helen Newman?	**Yes, I am.**
Are you working?	**No, I'm not.**
Is Carolyn home?	**Yes, she is.**
Is she sleeping?	**No, she's not.**
Am I a good singer?	**No, you're not.**
Am I singing a nice song?	**Yes, you are.**

Short answers with the present progressive are the same as short answers with the verb **be**. (See pages 36 and 42.)

 ## PRACTICE

Look at the pictures and answer yes or no.

EX. Is Linda speaking English?
▷ **Yes, she is.**

Are they dancing?
▷ **No, they're not.**

1. Are you playing the guitar?
▷

2. Are you singing?
▷

3. Is she speaking English?

4. Is Alice working?

5. Is the dog sleeping?

6. Are they reading the newspaper?

7. Are they speaking English?

8. Is he asking a question?

9. Are you eating?

10. Ask your own question.

STUDY 5

Information questions in the present progressive:
Where are you going?

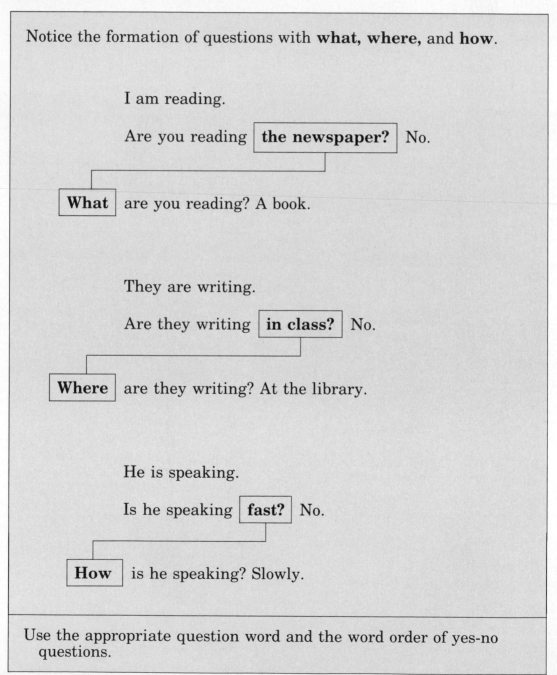

Notice the formation of questions with **what, where,** and **how**.

I am reading.

Are you reading the newspaper? No.

What are you reading? A book.

They are writing.

Are they writing in class? No.

Where are they writing? At the library.

He is speaking.

Is he speaking fast? No.

How is he speaking? Slowly.

Use the appropriate question word and the word order of yes-no
questions.

Notice the use of the question word **how**.

How is he speaking?   He's speaking **clearly**.
How am I singing?   You're singing **well**.
How are we going there? We're going there **by bus**.

To answer a question with **how**, use a phrase with **by** (**by bus, by car, by taxi**), or use an adverb. Some adverbs are short: **hard, fast, well.** Most adverbs are made by adding **-ly** to adjectives.

clear	**clearly**
quick	**quickly**
slow	**slowly**

PRECTICE

PRACTICE

A. Answer the questions. Look at the pictures and use the cues.

 well

EX. How is he singing?
 ⇩ **He's singing well**.

 quickly

1. How is she working?
 ⇩

 clearly

2. How are we speaking?
 ⇩

 hard

3. How am I studying?
 ⇩

 by car

4. How is she going to work?
 ⇩

 fast

5. How are we dancing?
 ⇩

B. Ask information questions with *what*, *where*, or *how*. Answer the questions.

EX. he studying/in the library
  ▷ **Where is he studying?**
     He's studying in the
     library.

    I speaking/very clearly
  ▷ **How am I speaking?**
     You're speaking very clearly.

1. Manuel sleeping/in a chair
  ▷

2. she drinking/coffee
  ▷

3. they eating/in a restaurant
  ▷

4. Yoko going/to France
  ▷

5. I dancing/very well
   ▷

6. they singing/very slowly
   ▷

7. you going to Miami/by bus
   ▷

8. she playing/the guitar
   ▷

9. they talking/in the bedroom
   ▷

10. Ask your own question.
    ▷

LISTEN

A. Look at the pictures below. Then listen to each sentence and write the letter of the sentence next to the matching picture.

1. _____

2. _____

3. _____

4. _____

THIS CLASS IS INTERESTING.

5. _____

6. _____

B. Listen to each question. Then choose the correct answer.

1. a. Yes. They're writing a letter.
   b. Yes. I'm reading.
   c. Yes, I am.

2. a. We're studying English.
   b. He's studying English.
   c. He's studying in Mexico.

3. a. Yes, we are.
   b. Yes, they are.
   c. Yes, you are.

4. a. I'm going home.
   b. You're going to New York.
   c. He's going home.

5. a. No, I'm not.
   b. No, he's not.
   c. No, they're not.

6. a. Yes. I'm listening to the radio.
   b. Yes. I'm teaching.
   c. Yes, I am.

SPEAK

A. Listen to the telephone conversation.

JIM:	Hello?
CARLOS:	Hello. Is Philip there?
JIM:	Yes, he is. Just a minute, please.
PHILIP:	Hello?
CARLOS:	Hi, Philip. This is Carlos.
PHILIP:	Oh, hi, Carlos. What are you doing?
CARLOS:	I'm watching TV. What about you?
PHILIP:	I'm studying.

B. Practice the conversation with two classmates. Use your own information.

STUDENT 1:	Hello?
STUDENT 2:	Hello. Is _____ there?
STUDENT 1:	Yes, he (she) is. Just a minute please.
STUDENT 3:	Hello?
STUDENT 2:	Hi, _____. This is _____.
STUDENT 3:	Oh, hi, _____. What are you doing?
STUDENT 2:	I'm _____. What about you?
STUDENT 3:	I'm _____.

C. Now close your book and practice the conversation with two different classmates.

READ

The Lewises at Home

It is eight o'clock and the Lewis family is very busy. Mr. and Mrs. Lewis are in the kitchen. Mrs. Lewis is washing the dishes, and Mr. Lewis is drying them. Donald Lewis is in the bedroom. He is doing math problems, and he is working hard. Lisa Lewis is playing the piano in the living room. She is practicing a very difficult song. Dennis Lewis is in the basement with a friend, Mark. They aren't studying. They are watching television.

Alan Lewis is leaving on a trip. He's a lawyer, and he's going to Boston. He's going by car.

Answer the questions.

1. Where is the Lewis family?
2. What are Mr. and Mrs. Lewis doing?
3. What is Donald doing?
4. Where is he studying?
5. Who is playing the piano?
6. Is she practicing an easy song?
7. Is she practicing in the basement?

Ask questions about Dennis, Mark, and Alan.

THINK

Work with a classmate or a small group. Ask and answer questions about the pictures.

1.

2.

3.

4.

PRONOUNCE: [s]

sip	voiceless, alveolar
	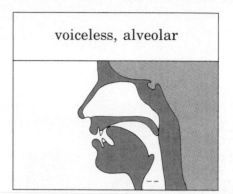

A. Repeat the words.

sing	Alice	Steve
sad	yes	sip
song	fast	soup

B. Repeat the sentences.

1. Alice is singing a sad song.
2. Vincent is sipping the soup fast.
3. Steve is a tourist in Boston.

C. On a sheet of paper, write the numbers of the words that have the sound [s].

1. it's	4. city	7. this	10. teachers	13. yes
2. sick	5. lawyers	8. soup	11. absent	14. Alice
3. Brazil	6. Vincent	9. sad	12. fast	15. Boston

CONVERSATION

Visiting a Friend

MRS. LEWIS: Hello.

STEVE: Hi. Is Dennis home?

MRS. LEWIS: I'm sorry. He's not here.

STEVE: Oh. Well, my name is Steve.

Please give him this book.

MRS. LEWIS: Sure. What's your last name,

Steve?

STEVE: Green. And thank you.

MRS. LEWIS: You're welcome.

INTERACTION

A. Make sentences like the models.

EX.   Dennis?   ⟡ **Is Dennis home?**
      not here.   **I'm sorry. He's not here.**

1. Lisa?   ⟡
    at school.

2. Donald?   ⟡
    at the store.

3. Mark and Alan?   ⟡
    at the library.

4. Mr. Lewis?   ⟡
    working.

5. Alice?   ⟡
    at the hospital.

6. Philip?   ⟡
    in class.

7. Mr. and Mrs. Newman?   ⟡
    not here.

8. Ask your own question.   ⟡

B. Make sentences like the models.

EX.　him/this book.
　▷　**Please give him this book.**
　　Sure.
　　Thank you.
　　You're welcome.

1.　me/a pencil.
　▷

2.　him/a piece of paper.
　▷

3.　her/a message.
　▷

4.　Alice/this pen.
　▷

5.　me/an apple.
　▷

STUDY 1

Requests: *Please study the lesson. Don't forget.*

Notice the form of the requests.

> AFFIRMATIVE
> Listen.
> Be quiet.
> Answer me.

Affirmative requests begin with the simple form of the verb (**listen, be, answer**).

> NEGATIVE
> Don't talk.
> Don't speak fast.
> Don't tell me.

Negative requests begin with **don't** (**do not**).

Notice the position of **please**.

> **Please** give me a pencil.
> Give me a pencil, **please**.
>
> **Please** don't forget.
> Don't forget, **please**.

Use **please** to make a polite request.

PRACTICE

Make a negative and an affirmative request, using the cues.

EX. open your book. ▷ **Please don't open your book.**
close your book. **Close your book, please.**
(Please close your book.)

1. read the newspaper. ▷
do your homework.

2. speak fast. ▷
speak slowly.

3. repeat the question. ▷
repeat the answer.

4. answer the telephone. ▷
answer the door.

5. sit on the floor. ▷
sit here.

6. forget. ▷
give him a message.

7. write with a pencil. ▷
write with a pen.

STUDY 2

Object pronouns: *Excuse me.*

Notice the object pronouns such as **me**, **him**, **her**, **us**.

I'm sorry.	Excuse	**me**.
Watch your brother.	Watch	**him**.
Ask Lynn.	Ask	**her**.
Write the lesson.	Write	**it**.
Tell Dennis and me.	Tell	**us**.
Open your books.	Open	**them**.

The object form of

I	is	me.
you		you.
he		him.
she		her.
it		it.
we		us.
you		you.
they		them.

PRACTICE

Make requests using the correct object pronoun.

EX. The door is open.
Please close __it__.

1. George is in the hospital.
Please visit _____.

2. The lessons are difficult.
Please study _____.

3. I'm singing.
Please listen to _____.

4. The saleswoman is here.
Please ask _____.

5. Helen and I are dancing.
Please watch _____.

6. The book is very good.
Please read _____.

7. Toshi is an important man.
Please talk to _____.

STUDY 3

Verbs with two objects: *Please give him this book.*

Notice the position of the two objects.

| Give | | the pencil | **to me.** |

| Give | **me** | the pencil. |

| Write | | a letter | **to him.** |

| Write | **him** | a letter. |

Use **to** with the object pronoun after a direct object.
  Give the pencil to me.

Omit **to** with the object pronoun before a direct object.
  Give me the pencil.

PRACTICE

A. Look at the pictures and change the model sentence to fit each picture.

EX.   Please **give me the map**.

1.   Please _____.

2.   Please _____.

3.   Please _____.

B. Look at the pictures and use the cues. Make polite requests with and without *to*.

EX. give/him
   ↳ **Please give the pen to him.**
     What?
     Please give him the pen.

1. read/her
  ↳

2. give/me
  ↳

3. read/them
  ↳

4. write/him
  ↳

5. give/them
  ↳

STUDY 4

The colors: *red, yellow, blue, . . .*

Learn the names of the colors.

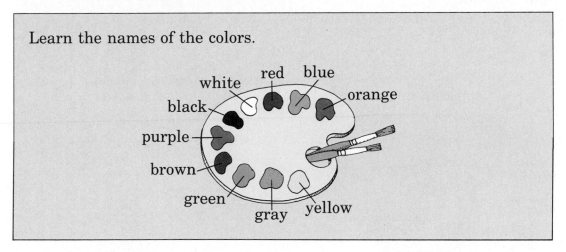

PRACTICE

A. Make sentences. Tell the color of each item.

EX.   strawberries
⇨   **The strawberries are red**.

1.   pear
⇨

2.   grapes
⇨

3.   potatoes
⇨

4.   orange
⇨

5.   bananas
⇨

B. Complete each sentence with an appropriate color adjective.

EX.   He's wearing a **white** shirt.

1.   They're wearing _____ coats.

2.   He's buying a _____ hat.

3.   She's painting a _____ flower.

4.   They're eating _____ apples.

5.   She's wearing _____ shoes.

6.   He's driving a _____ car.

7.   She's giving him an _____ book.

C. Look at the pictures. Ask and answer questions using the cues.

EX. wearing?
  ▷ **What is he wearing?**
     He's wearing a green shirt.

1. eating?
  ▷

2. wearing?
  ▷

3. buying?
  ▷

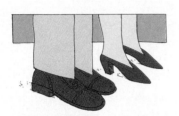

4. painting?
  ▷

5. giving her?
  ▷

6. eating?
  ▷

7. driving?
  ▷

STUDY 5

Questions about colors: *What color is the house?*

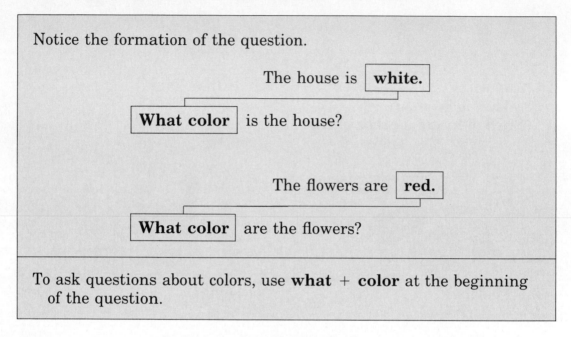

Notice the formation of the question.

The house is | white.

| What color | is the house?

The flowers are | red.

| What color | are the flowers?

To ask questions about colors, use **what** + **color** at the beginning of the question.

 # PRACTICE

What color is each of the things in the picture? Ask and answer questions using the cues.

EX. clouds?   ⇩ **What color are the clouds?**
                                           They're white.

1. sky?   ⇩

2. house?   ⇩

3. door?   ⇩

4. flowers?   ⇩

5. grass?   ⇩

6. trees?   ⇩

7. chairs?   ⇩

8. car?   ⇩

9. cat?   ⇩

10. Ask questions about things   ⇩
      in the classroom.

LISTEN

A. Listen and write the conversation.

1. _____ ?
2. _____ . _____ .
3. _____ ?
4. _____ . _____ .
5. _____ ? _____ ?
6. ___ . _____ .

B. Listen to the paragraph. Then complete the sentences.

1. Steve and Carlos
   a. are in English class.
   b. are in math class.
   c. aren't in math class.

2. They are
   a. studying hard.
   b. not studying hard.
   c. going home now.

3. The class is
   a. interesting.
   b. not interesting.
   c. easy.

4. The red math book is
   a. easy.
   b. difficult.
   c. big.

SPEAK

A. Listen to the conversation.

STEVE: Hi. Is Dennis home?

LISA: No, he's not.

STEVE: Well, please give him this letter.

LISA: Sure.

STEVE: Uh . . . Please don't forget. It's important.

LISA: O.K. What's your name?

STEVE: Steve.

LISA: What's your last name?

STEVE: Green. My name's Steve Green.

B. Practice the conversation with a classmate. Use your own information.

STUDENT 1: Hi. Is _____ home?

STUDENT 2: No, he's (she's) not.

STUDENT 1: Well, please give him (her) _____.

STUDENT 2: Sure.

STUDENT 1: Please don't forget. It's (they're) important.

STUDENT 2: O.K. What's your name?

STUDENT 1: _____.

STUDENT 2: What's your last name?

STUDENT 1: _____. My name's _____ _____.

C. Now close your book and practice the conversation with a different classmate.

READ

Dear Maria,

How are you? My family and I are fine. My brother Robert and my sister Sally are in college now. Robert is studying languages, and he is doing well. Sally is studying very hard. She's taking chemistry, and it's a difficult subject.

I'm studying hard, too. I'm in high school. I'm taking science, math, history, English, and Spanish. My favorite subject is math. It's interesting. My teacher is very good, and the book is easy. Also, I'm on the soccer team. Soccer is exciting, and the team is very good.

What are you doing? Please write me a long letter and send me pictures of you and your family. Please give your family my love.

Your friend,

Richard

A. Answer by marking TRUE (T) or FALSE (F).

1. Richard, Robert, and Sally are fine.	T	F
2. Richard, Robert, and Sally are in college.	T	F
3. Robert is studying languages.	T	F
4. Sally is studying languages, too.	T	F
5. Richard is studying very hard.	T	F
6. Richard is taking chemistry.	T	F
7. Math is interesting.	T	F
8. Richard is on the soccer team.	T	F

B. Answer these questions about yourself.

1. What's your favorite subject or class?
2. Is it easy or difficult?
3. Are you studying hard?
4. How's the book?

THINK

What is wrong with the pictures?

1.

2.

PRONOUNCE: [z], [s]

zip: [z]	sip: [s]

A. Repeat the words and contrast [z] and [s].

please	memorize	easy	music	Rose	songs
lesson	students	class	tourists	sit	sing

B. Repeat the sentences.

1. Please memorize the lesson.
2. Is the lesson easy?
3. Yes, it is.

4. This is a music class.
5. The students are singing songs.
6. Rose and Susan are sitting in this class.

C. On a sheet of paper, write *a* for the sound [z] and *b* for the sound [s].

1. it's
2. city
3. busy
4. sick
5. Rose

6. easy
7. teachers
8. class
9. he's
10. practice

CONVERSATION

Talking about Occupations

CARLOS: Tina Brown is a translator.

She speaks English and Chinese.

DONALD: Really?

CARLOS: Yes. She works at the

United Nations.

DONALD: My brother works at the

United Nations, too.

CARLOS: Is he a translator?

DONALD: No. He's a guide.

He works there on the weekend.

CARLOS: Tina works there every day.

109

INTERACTION

A. Make sentences like the models. Use the cues.

EX. Tina Brown/translator.
     at the United Nations.
  ▷ **Tina Brown is a translator.**
     Really?
     Yes. She works at the United Nations.

1. Alice Garcia/nurse.
    in a hospital.
  ▷

2. Peter Sato/factory worker.
    in an auto factory.
  ▷

3. Bob Ogawa/waiter.
    at Pierre's Café.
  ▷

4. Talk about a classmate.
  ▷

B. Make sentences like the models. Use the cues.

EX. my brother/at the United
Nations.
translator?
guide.

⇨ **My brother works at the United
Nations.
Is he a translator?
No, he's a guide.**

1. Julia/in a hospital.
nurse?
doctor.

⇨

2. George/in a school.
teacher?
secretary.

⇨

3. Helen/in a garage.
mechanic?
bookkeeper.

⇨

4. Bob/in a restaurant.
cook?
waiter.

⇨

5. Mrs. Lewis /in an office.
secretary?
computer programmer.

⇨

6. Talk about a classmate.

⇨

STUDY 1

Regular present tense: *She works at the United Nations.*

Notice the verb forms.

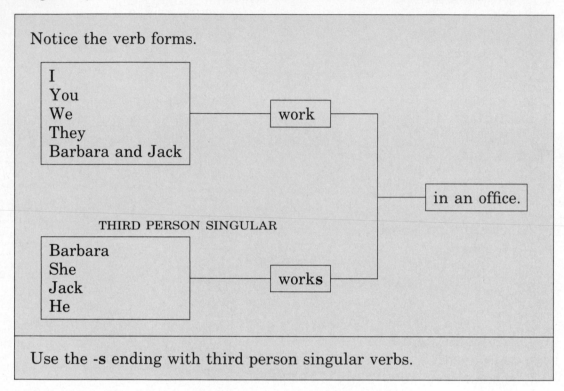

Use the **-s** ending with third person singular verbs.

PRACTICE

A. Look at the pictures and complete the sentences. Use the cues.

EX. I'm a teacher. (teach)
I **teach** geography.

He's a mechanic. (repair)
He **repairs** cars in a garage.

1. We're students. (study)
   We _____ geography.

2. She's a singer. (sing)
   She _____ in a club.

3. They're musicians. (play)
   They _____ the guitar.

4. He's a waiter. (work)
   He _____ in a restaurant.

5. I'm a scientist. (work)
   I _____ in a laboratory.

6. Jane is a saleswoman. (sell)
   She _____ clothes in a store.

7. We're cooks. (cook)
   We _____ food in a
   restaurant.

8. They're computer
   programmers. (work)
   They _____ in an office.

B. Look at the pictures. Using the cues, make sentences about the people.

EX. Lisa/play/every day
　▷ **Lisa plays the piano every day.**

1. Carlos/walk/every morning
　▷

2. I/sleep/every night
　▷

3. We/play/every afternoon
　▷

4. He/write/every week
　▷

5. They/swim/every week
　▷

6. You/drink/in the morning
   ⇨

7. We/watch/in the evening
   ⇨

8. They/read/on the weekend
   ⇨

9. Linda/ride/every day
   ⇨

10. Tell about a classmate.
    ⇨

11. Tell about yourself.
    ⇨

STUDY 2

Third person singular of present tense:
He reads. She speaks. It changes.

Notice the pronunciation of the third person singular.

1. Pronounce [z] after all vowel sounds and all voiced final consonants [b, d, g, m, r, etc.] except those in group 3 below.

   The third person singular of

listen	is	listens.
read		reads.
study		studies.
swim		swims.

   Spelling: Notice that verbs ending in a consonant + **-y** take the ending **-ies (study – studies)**.

2. Pronounce [s] after the voiceless final sounds [p, t, k, f, θ].

   The third person singular of

stop	is	stops.
speak		speaks.
write		writes.

3. Pronounce [iz] after the final sounds [s, z, š, ž, č, ǰ].

   The third person singular of

practice	is	practices.
memorize		memorizes.
wash		washes.
relax		relaxes.
change		changes.

   Spelling: Notice that verbs ending in **-sh**, **-ch** , **-s**, **-z**, and **-x** take the ending **-es (wash – washes, relax – relaxes)**.

Learn these irregular verb forms.

The third person singular of

have	is	has.	[hæz]
go		goes.	[gowz]
do		does.	[dəz]

PRACTICE

Tina Brown works hard all day at the United Nations. After work she goes home. Say what she does after work.

EX. change her clothes
  ▷ **She changes her clothes.**

1. sit down
  ▷

2. read the newspaper
  ▷

3. cook dinner
  ▷

4. eat dinner
  ▷

5. do the dishes
  ▷

6. watch the news
  ▷

7. go to bed
  ▷

STUDY 3

The days of the week: *Sunday, Monday, . . .*

Memorize the days of the week.

Sunday Monday Tuesday Wednesday Thursday Friday Saturday

 # PRACTICE

A. Look at the pictures and complete the sentences. Use the cues.

 type

 swim

EX. I __**type on Monday**__ .

1. He _____
_____ .

 shop

 play tennis

2. We _____
_____ .

3. I _____
_____ .

 go

 wash clothes

4. They _____
_____ .

5. She _____
_____ .

B. David Taylor is a college student. On the weekend, he works at the United Nations. Look at the calendar and say what he does after school and on the weekend.

	AUGUST				AUGUST		
SUN.	MON.	TUES.	WED.	THURS.	FRI.	SAT.	NOTES
	swim at pool 1	practice the guitar 2	study Portuguese 3	play tennis with Donald 4	morning have a guitar lesson afternoon wash clothes 5	morning shop for food 6	
evening go to the movies with Tina 7	swim 8	guitar practice 9	Portuguese lesson 10	tennis with Donald 11	morning guitar lesson afternoon wash clothes 12	morning food shopping 13	
evening movies with Tina 14	15	16	17	18	19	20	

EX. Monday
⇩ **He swims on Monday.**

1. Tuesday
⇩

2. Wednesday
⇩

3. Thursday
⇩

4. Friday morning
⇩

5. Friday afternoon
⇩

6. Saturday morning
⇩

7. Sunday evening
⇩

LISTEN

A. Look at the story quickly. Try to guess the missing words, but don't write them. Then listen and fill in the blanks.

Maria and Laura _____ _____ Italy, but they _____ to school _____ Washington, D.C. _____ study English _____ Monday, _____, and Friday. They _____ and _____ English very well. They _____ English well, _____. Maria _____ Laura practice English _____ day. They _____ in American stores, and _____ eat in American restaurants. Also, they _____ to American movies.

B. Listen to each sentence. Then choose an appropriate response.

1. a. She speaks Spanish, too.
   b. She doesn't speak Spanish.
   c. She speaks English, too.

2. a. This is Ann and this is Jim.
   b. Yes. They work at the United Nations.
   c. The United Nations is big.

3. a. Yes. He's from Greece.
   b. Yes. He's handsome.
   c. Yes. He's in New York now.

4. a. I'm a secretary.
   b. Really? Are you secretaries?
   c. She's a secretary.

5. a. They're teachers.
   b. They play tennis every day, too.
   c. They teach every day.

6. a. I take science and math.
   b. I'm a student.
   c. I have classes every day.

SPEAK

A. Listen to the conversation.

TINA: What's your occupation?
DONALD: I'm a student.
TINA: Really?
DONALD: Yes. I study at the School of Arts and Sciences. What about you?
TINA: I work in an office.
DONALD: Are you a secretary?
TINA: No. I'm a translator.

B. Practice the conversation with a classmate. Use your own information.

STUDENT 1: What's your occupation?
STUDENT 2: I'm a (an) _____ .
STUDENT 1: Really?
STUDENT 2: Yes. I study (work) _____ . What about you?
STUDENT 1: I work (study) _____ .
STUDENT 2: Are you a (an) _____ ?
STUDENT 1: _____ . I'm a (an) _____ .

C. Now close your book and practice the conversation with a different classmate.

READ

Foreign Languages Lead to Interesting Jobs at the United Nations

Tina Brown, David Taylor, and Robert Owen all speak foreign languages and have interesting jobs at the United Nations.

Tina Brown speaks Chinese fluently. She is a translator at the U.N. She translates letters from Chinese to English. She speaks Chinese all day at the office. After work she goes home and relaxes. She reads newspapers and watches television—in English.

David Taylor speaks Portuguese. He is a guide at the U.N. He gives tours to Portuguese and Brazilian tourists. He works on weekends. During the week Mr. Taylor is a student. He's studying business. He also plays the guitar, swims, and plays tennis.

Robert Owen speaks Spanish. He isn't a translator, and he isn't a guide. He manages the bookstore. He sells books about different countries and cultures. Mr. Owen is a singer, too. On the weekend, he sings in a club. He sings in English and Spanish, and he plays the guitar.

Check the right boxes.

	Robert Owen	Tina Brown	David Taylor
1. is a translator			
2. is a manager			
3. is a guide			
4. speaks English			
5. speaks Chinese			
6. speaks Spanish			
7. watches TV			
8. sings			
9. plays the guitar			
10. plays tennis			

THINK

A. This is Donald Day's busy calendar. Work with a classmate or a small group. Give information about Donald Day.

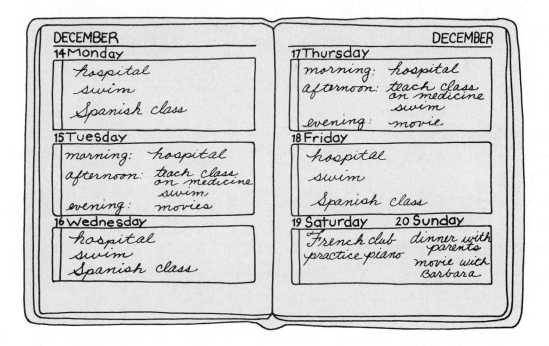

DECEMBER   DECEMBER

14 Monday
- hospital
- swim
- Spanish class

15 Tuesday
- morning: hospital
- afternoon: teach class on medicine / swim
- evening: movies

16 Wednesday
- hospital
- swim
- Spanish class

17 Thursday
- morning: hospital
- afternoon: teach class on medicine / swim
- evening: movie

18 Friday
- hospital
- swim
- Spanish class

19 Saturday
- French club
- practice piano

20 Sunday
- dinner with parents
- movie with Barbara

B. Give your own information to a classmate or a group.

Give your name.

Give your occupation.

Say what you do at work or school.

Say what you do after work and on the weekend.

PRONOUNCE: [d]

day

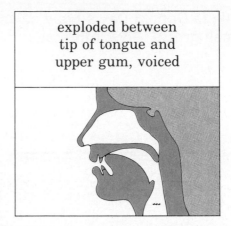

exploded between
tip of tongue and
upper gum, voiced

A. Repeat the words.

day	**D**onal**d**	**d**octor	**d**ifficult	Lon**d**on
har**d**	**D**avi**d**	**d**oing	me**d**icine	stu**d**y

B. Repeat the sentences.

1. Is Donald a doctor?
2. Yes, he's a doctor of medicine.
3. He's Donald Day, M.D.
4. He's Dr. Donald Day.
5. Where is David Day?
6. David is in London.
7. What is David doing in London?
8. He's studying difficult subjects.

CONVERSATION

Shopping for Food

JACK: Helen, do you want fish or meat?

HELEN: I want fish. I don't like meat.

JACK: Do we have potatoes?

HELEN: No, we don't.

We need potatoes and tomatoes.

JACK: Do we need coffee?

HELEN: Yes, we do.

JACK: How about soda?

HELEN: No. We have soda at home.

125

INTERACTION

A. Ask questions using the cues, and answer with personal information.

EX.   fish or meat?
  ▷   **Do you want fish or meat?**
      I want fish (meat). I don't like
      meat (fish).

1.   coffee or tea?
  ▷

2.   milk or cream?
  ▷

3.   rice or French fries?
  ▷

4.   soda or water?
  ▷

5.   Ask your own question.
  ▷

B. Make sentences like the models. Use the cues.

EX. coffee?
 ⇨ **Do we need coffee?**
    No, we don't. We have coffee at home.

1. milk?
 ⇨

2. sugar?
 ⇨

3. meat?
 ⇨

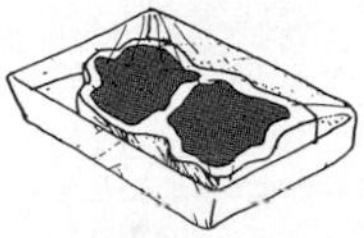

4. potatoes?
 ⇨

5. bread?
 ⇨

6. eggs?
 ⇨

7. Ask your own question.
 ⇨

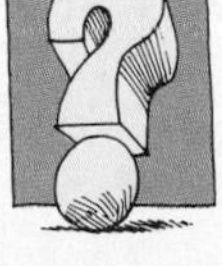

STUDY 1

Negative statements in the present tense: *I don't like meat.*

Compare the affirmative and negative statements.

AFFIRMATIVE
I like coffee.
He likes tea.

NEGATIVE

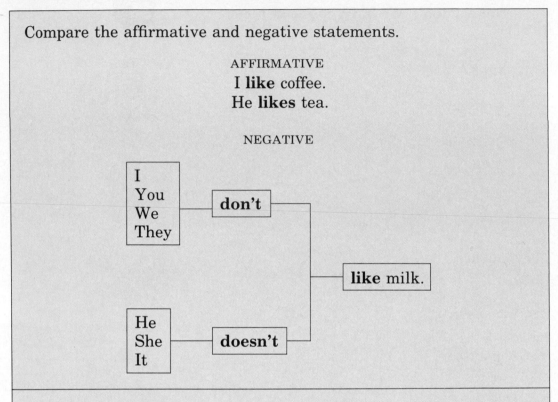

For negative statements, use **don't** and **doesn't** with the simple form of the verb: **eat**, **drink**, **like**, and so forth.
Don't and **doesn't** are the contractions of **do not** and **does not**.

PRACTICE

Complete each sentence using the negative.

EX.   Jack likes meat, but Helen <u>**doesn't like meat**</u>.

1. Steve works in the supermarket, but Jack and Helen
   _____.

2. You drink coffee, but I _____.

3. I like milk, but Helen _____.

4. Cats eat fish, but dogs _____.

5. Carol speaks Spanish, but Linda
   _____.

6. Alice works in a hospital, but Tina and David
   _____.

7. David has a job, but Donald _____.

8. Carolyn teaches math, but Mr. and Mrs. Jackson
   _____.

9. I like movies, but my sister _____.

10. Make your own sentence. _____.

STUDY 2

Yes-no questions in the present tense: *Do we need coffee?*

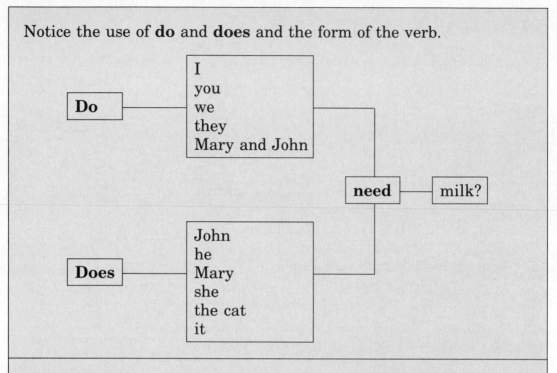

Notice the use of **do** and **does** and the form of the verb.

Do	I you we they Mary and John	
		need — milk?
Does	John he Mary she the cat it	

Use **does** with the third person singular: **he**, **she**, **it**, **John**, and so forth.

Use the simple form of the verb, **need**, **want**, **like**, and so forth, with both **do** and **does**.

 # PRACTICE

A. Look at the pictures. Then ask questions with the verb *like* and answer using affirmative statements.

 milk

 meat

EX. Somsak
   ▷ **Does Somsak like milk?**
   Yes. He likes milk.

Donald and David
▷ **Do Donald and David like meat?**
Yes. They like meat.

1. Bill
⇨

2. they
⇨

cats

fish

3. you
⇨

4. Lynn
⇨

ice cream

cake

5. Eve
⇨

6. you and Francis
⇨

New York

7. Tina and David
⇨

8. Linda
⇨

B. Ask questions with *want* and the cues. Look at the pictures and answer the questions.

EX. you/tea or coffee?
  ⇩ **Do you want tea or coffee?**
  I want tea.

1. he/water or milk?
  ⇩

2. she/coffee or tea?
  ⇩

3. they/soda or milk?
  ⇩

4. you/fish or chicken?
  ⇩

5. Helen/rice or potatoes?
  ⇩

6. Jack and Helen/fish or meat?
   ⇨

7. you and Helen/soup or salad?
   ⇨

8. you and Philip/water or milk?
   ⇨

9. the cat/fish or meat?
   ⇨

10. you/a pear or an orange?
    ⇨

11. Ask a classmate a question.
    ⇨

STUDY 3

Short answers in the present tense: *Yes, we do. No, we don't.*

Notice the affirmative and negative short answers.

Do you speak Japanese?	**Yes, I do.**
Does she work in Japan?	**Yes, she does.**
Do they work on weekends?	**No, they don't.**
Does he play tennis?	**No, he doesn't.**

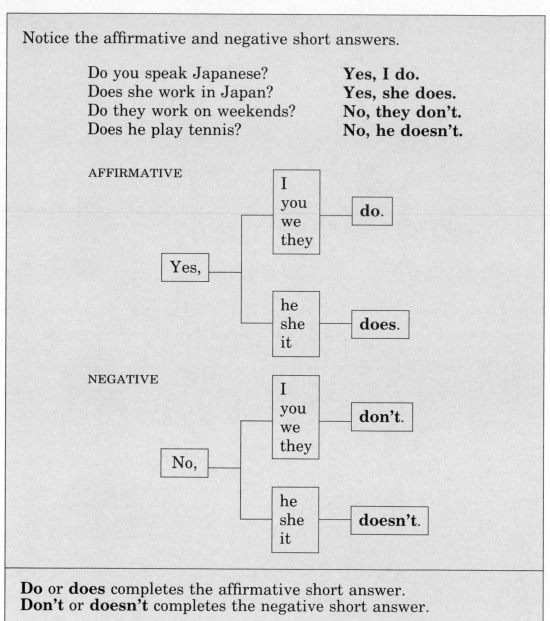

AFFIRMATIVE

Yes,
I you we they **do**.
he she it **does**.

NEGATIVE

No,
I you we they **don't**.
he she it **doesn't**.

Do or **does** completes the affirmative short answer.
Don't or **doesn't** completes the negative short answer.

PRACTICE

Look at the pictures. Answer the questions with affirmative or negative short answers.

EX. Do Tina and David work
     at the United Nations?
 ▷ **Yes, they do.**

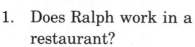

1. Does Ralph work in a
    restaurant?
 ▷

2. Does Carlos study
    English?
 ▷

3. Does Yoko like art?
 ▷

4. Do cats drink tea?
 ▷

5. Ask your own question.
 ▷

LISTEN

A. Look at the pictures below. Then listen to each sentence and write the letter of the sentence next to the matching picture.

1. _____

2. _____

3. _____

4. _____

5. _____

6. _____

B. Listen and write the questions and answers.

1. _____?

   _____.

2. _____?

   _____.

3. _____?

   _____.

SPEAK

A. Listen to the conversation.

DONALD: Hi, Carlos.

CARLOS: Hello, Donald. Come in.

DONALD: What are you doing?

CARLOS: I'm cooking. Are you hungry?

DONALD: Well, yes, I am.

CARLOS: Then stay for dinner.

DONALD: O.K. Thank you.

CARLOS: Do you like fish?

DONALD: Yes, I do.

CARLOS: Good. Do you want rice or
potatoes with your fish?

DONALD: Oh, potatoes, I think.

B. Practice the conversation with a classmate. Use your own information.

STUDENT 1: Hi, _____.

STUDENT 2: Hello, _____. Come in.

STUDENT 1: What are you doing?

STUDENT 2: I'm cooking. Are you hungry?

STUDENT 1: Well, yes, I am.

STUDENT 2: Then stay for _____.

STUDENT 1: O.K. Thank you.

STUDENT 2: Do you like _____?

STUDENT 1: Yes, I do.

STUDENT 2: Good. Do you want _____ or _____
with your _____?

STUDENT 1: Oh, _____, I think.

C. Now close your book and practice the conversation with a different classmate.

READ

Dinner in New York

The Blue Room is a famous restaurant in New York. The food is excellent, and the waiters and waitresses are polite and friendly.

Hector and Isabel Rivera are having dinner at the Blue Room. The Riveras are from Venezuela. They are tourists in the United States. They speak Spanish, but they speak English well, too. Mrs. Rivera is ordering soup, fish, and rice. She likes fish, and it is very good at the Blue Room. Mr. Rivera does not like fish. He prefers meat. He is ordering soup, steak, and potatoes. He also wants coffee with dinner. Mrs. Rivera drinks coffee after dinner. She likes water with dinner.

The Riveras are having a good time. They like American food, and they like the Blue Room restaurant. The waitress is nice, and they like her, too.

Answer the questions.

1. Is the Blue Room famous?
2. Is the food bad?
3. What about the waiters and waitresses?
4. Where are the Riveras from?
5. What are they doing in the United States?
6. What is Mrs. Rivera ordering?
7. Does Mr. Rivera like fish?
8. Do Mr. and Mrs. Rivera drink coffee with dinner?
9. Are Mr. and Mrs. Rivera having a good time?
10. Do they like the waitress?

THINK

Interview the people in your classroom, and complete the chart. Write the name of one person in each blank.

FOOD
Who likes American food?
Who likes coffee?
Who likes tea?
Who likes fish? Meat?
FREE TIME
Who likes movies?
Who likes art?
Who likes soccer?
Who likes music?
WORK
Who studies hard?
Who wants a job in an office?
Who has a job in an office?
Who thinks English is difficult?

PRONOUNCE: [ð]

they

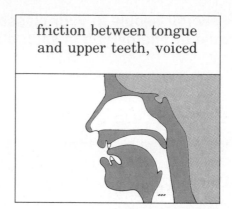

friction between tongue and upper teeth, voiced

A. Repeat the words.

this	**th**ey	**th**e
fa**th**er	mo**th**er	bro**th**er

B. Repeat the sentences.

1. Is this the father?
2. Yes. This is the father.

3. Is this the mother?
4. Yes. This is the mother.

5. Are they the brothers?
6. Yes. The brothers are next
   to their mother and father.

C. On a sheet of paper, write the numbers of the words that have the sound [ð].

1. mother	3. Athens	5. the	7. brother
2. this	4. father	6. with	8. they

CONVERSATION

Sightseeing

HELEN: Excuse me. Is there a post office near here?

OFFICER: Yes, there is. It's on Main Street.

JACK: And where's the Museum of Art?

OFFICER: That's the Museum of Art over there.

HELEN: And what's this?

OFFICER: This is the library.

HELEN: Thank you.

OFFICER: You're welcome.

INTERACTION

A. Make sentences like the models. Use the cues.

EX. post office?
on Main Street.

↪ **Excuse me. Is there a post
office near here?
Yes, there is. It's on Main Street.**

1. library?
on White Street.

↪

2. bus station?
on Oak Street.

↪

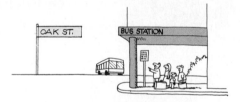

3. bank?
on Washington Avenue.

↪

4. subway station?
on Green Street.

↪

5. Ask your own question.

↪

B. Make sentences like the models. Use the cues.

EX. the sports stadium?
     over there.
   ▷ **Where's the sports stadium?**
     That's the sports stadium
     over there.

     the National Bank?
     right here.
   ▷ **Where's the National Bank?**
     This is the National Bank
     right here.

1.   the Museum of Art?
     over there.
   ▷

2.   the post office?
     right here.
   ▷

3.   the library?
     over there.
   ▷

4.   the supermarket?
     right here.
   ▷

STUDY 1

Demonstrative pronouns:
This is the library. That's the Museum of Art over there.

Notice the use of **this, that, these,** and **those**.

SINGULAR   **This** is an apple.   **That** is a banana.

PLURAL   **These** are apples.   **Those** are bananas.

This and **these** are used for objects near the speaker.
That and **those** are used for objects away from the speaker.

 # PRACTICE

A. Look at the pictures. The objects are not near you. Point out the objects using *that* or *those*.

▷ **That's a hot dog.**

EX.

▷ **Those are apples.**

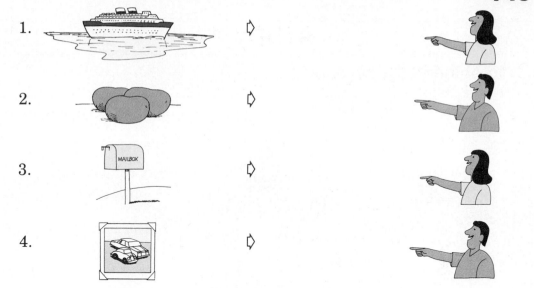

1.
2.
3.
4.

B. Look at the pictures. The objects are near you. Answer the questions with *this* or *these*.

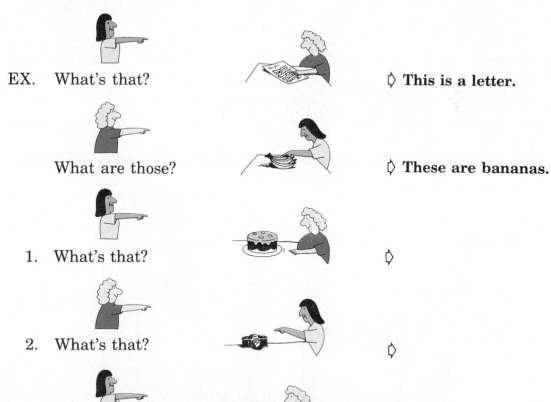

EX.   What's that?   ▷ **This is a letter.**

What are those?   ▷ **These are bananas.**

1.   What's that?   ▷

2.   What's that?   ▷

3.   What are those?   ▷

STUDY 2

Parts of the body: *arms, legs, . . .*

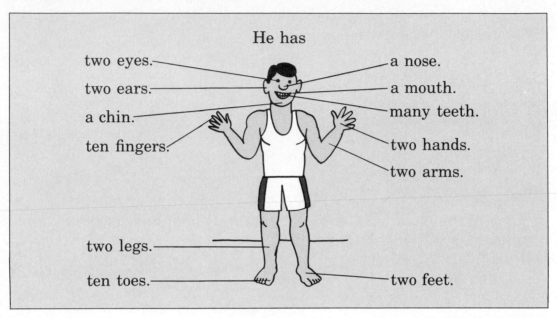

He has

two eyes.
two ears.
a chin.
ten fingers.

a nose.
a mouth.
many teeth.
two hands.
two arms.

two legs.
ten toes.

two feet.

PRACTICE

Point to the parts of the body in Study 2. Ask and answer questions.

EX. What's this?
  ▷ **This is a nose.**

  What are these?
  ▷ **These are feet.**

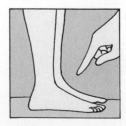

STUDY 3

Irregular plurals: *These are children.*

Learn these irregular plurals.

The plural of

man	is	men.
woman		women.
child		children.
foot		feet.
tooth		teeth.
person		people.

PRACTICE

Give a sentence in the singular. Then make the sentence plural.

EX. ▷ **This is a tooth.**   ▷ **These are teeth.**

 person

1. ▷    ▷

 woman

2. ▷   ▷

 man

3. ▷   ▷

STUDY 4

Numbers 1 to 20: *one, two, three, . . .*

Learn these numbers.

1	one	11	eleven
2	two	12	twelve
3	three	13	thirteen
4	four	14	fourteen
5	five	15	fifteen
6	six	16	sixteen
7	seven	17	seventeen
8	eight	18	eighteen
9	nine	19	nineteen
10	ten	20	twenty

Stress the last syllable of numbers ending in **-teen**: thir**teen**, four**teen**, and so forth.

PRACTICE

A. Count from one to twenty.

B. Read these numbers aloud.

a. 5, 10, 15, 20   c. 3, 6, 9, 12

b. 2, 4, 8, 16   d. 1, 7, 11, 13

C. Read these problems.

EX.   5 + 5 = 10
       5 and 5 is 10.

a. 2 + 2 = 4   c. 7 + 11 = 18   e. 8 + 8 = 16

b. 9 + 3 = 12   d. 10 + 10 = 20   f. 10 + 3 = 13

STUDY 5

There is/there are: *There is a post office on Main Street.*

Notice the use of **there is** and **there are** to tell about the picture below.

There is	a	cat	on the table.
There's	a	cake	on the table.
There are	(two)	glasses	on the table.
There are	(three)	plates	on the table.

There is is followed by a singular noun.
There are is followed by a plural noun.
After the noun, there is usually a phrase like **on the table**, which answers the question **where**.
There's is the contraction of **there is**.

 # PRACTICE

What is in each picture? Complete the sentences.

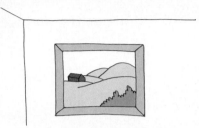

EX. <u>**There's a picture**</u> on the wall.

<u>**There are (two) eggs**</u> on the plate.

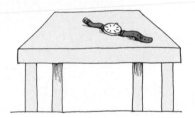

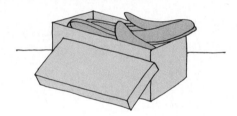

1. _____ on the table.

2. _____ in the box.

3. _____ in the basket.

4. _____ on the floor.

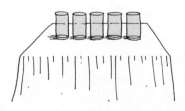

5. _____ on the chair.

6. _____ on the table.

STUDY 6

Questions with **there is/there are:**
Is there a picture on the wall?

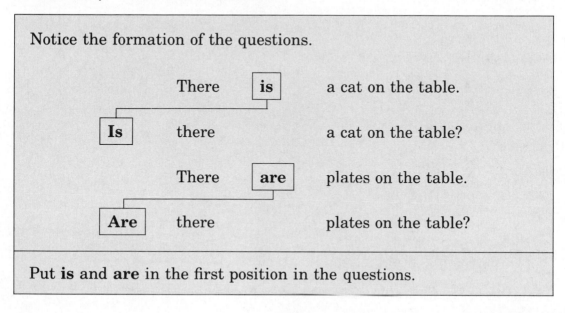

Notice the formation of the questions.

There	**is**	a cat on the table.
Is	there	a cat on the table?
There	**are**	plates on the table.
Are	there	plates on the table?

Put **is** and **are** in the first position in the questions.

PRACTICE

Jack and Helen Newman are visiting Washington, D.C., and they have a lot of questions. Ask questions about Washington, using the cues.

EX. subway?   ▷ **Is there a subway in Washington?**

      buses?   ▷ **Are there buses in Washington?**

1. art museums?   ▷

2. good theaters? ⇨

3. park? ⇨

4. nice hotels? ⇨

5. good restaurants? ⇨

6. a sports stadium? ⇨

7. interesting people? ⇨

8. nice stores? ⇨

STUDY 7

Short answers with **there is/there are**:
Yes, there is. No, there isn't.

Notice the short answers to the questions below.

Is there an art museum in Washington? **Yes, there is.**
Is there an art museum in Vale? **No, there isn't.**
Are there theaters in Washington? **Yes, there are.**
Are there theaters in Vale? **No, there aren't.**

Isn't is the contraction of **is not**.
Aren't is the contraction of **are not**.

PRACTICE

Jack and Helen Newman have a friend from Vale, Ohio. They are asking the friend about Vale. Ask and answer questions about the picture.

EX. hospital?
　▷ **Is there a hospital in Vale?**
　　No, there isn't.

5. school?
　▷

1. houses?
　▷

6. restaurants?
　▷

2. college?
　▷

7. park?
　▷

3. supermarket?
　▷

8. factories?
　▷

4. taxis?
　▷

9. Ask about something else.
　▷

STUDY 8

The contractions **isn't** and **aren't**: *We aren't working.*

Notice the possible contractions of **be** + **not**.

I am not busy now.	I'm not busy now.
We are not working.	We're not working.
	We **aren't** working.
She is not here.	She's not here.
	She **isn't** here.

Notice the short answers.

Are you hungry?	No, I'm not.
Are they eating?	No, they're not.
	No, they **aren't**.
Is he unhappy?	No, he's not.
	No, he **isn't**.

Are not is often contracted to **aren't**.
Is not is often contracted to **isn't**.
I am not has only one contraction: **I'm not**.
Aren't and **isn't** are often used in short answers.

 PRACTICE

Answer the questions with negative short answers. Use *'m not*, *isn't*, and *aren't*.

EX. Is Helen Newman in Chicago now?
⟡ **No, she isn't.**

Are Helen and Jack at home this week?
⟡ **No, they aren't.**

1. Is Jack Newman in Los Angeles?
    ⇩

2. Are Helen and Jack visiting Vale now?
    ⇩

3. Is Vale a big city?
    ⇩

4. Are there factories in Vale?
    ⇩

5. Is there an art museum in Vale?
    ⇩

6. Is Washington, D.C. a small town?
    ⇩

7. Are you visiting Washington, D.C. this week?
    ⇩

8. Are Washington and Vale in Canada?
    ⇩

9. Are you and your classmates tourists?
    ⇩

10. Am I going to Chicago this week?
    ⇩

11. Is there a museum in your city?
    ⇩

12. Are you studying art?
    ⇩

13. Ask your own question.
    ⇩

LISTEN

A. Look at the pictures below. Then listen to each sentence and write the letter of the sentence next to the matching picture.

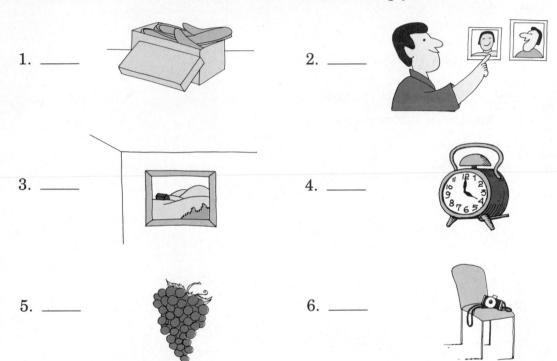

1. _____

2. _____

3. _____

4. _____

5. _____

6. _____

B. Listen to each question. Then choose the correct answer.

1. a. It's a child.
   b. It's a man.
   c. It's a cat.

2. a. It's a woman.
   b. It's a dog.
   c. It's a fish.

3. a. They're chairs.
   b. It's a chair.
   c. There's a chair.

4. a. It's a foot.
   b. It's an arm.
   c. It's a hand.

5. a. It's a leg.
   b. It's a hand.
   c. It's an arm.

6. a. They're pictures.
   b. It's a picture.
   c. There are pictures.

7. a. Yes, it is.
   b. Yes, there are.
   c. Yes, there is.

8. a. Yes, there is.
   b. No, there aren't.
   c. No, there isn't.

SPEAK

A. Listen to the conversation.

JACK:	Excuse me. Where's the museum?
OFFICER:	That's the museum over there.
JACK:	And is there a library near here?
OFFICER:	Yes, there is. There's a library on Main Street.
JACK:	What about a post office?
OFFICER:	I'm sorry. I don't know.

B. Practice the conversation with a classmate. Use your own information.

STUDENT 1: Excuse me. Where's the _____?

STUDENT 2: That's the _____ over there.

STUDENT 1: And is there a _____ near here?

STUDENT 2: Yes, there is. There's a _____ on
_____ Street.
(No, there isn't.)

STUDENT 1: What about a _____?

STUDENT 2: I'm sorry. I don't know.
(There's a _____ on _____ Street.)

C. Now close your book and practice the conversation with a different classmate.

An Interview with Doris Thurston
–Susan Blake

SUSAN: Tonight we are in Washington, D.C., and we are visiting the National Museum of Art. This is the museum guide, Doris Thurston. Doris, please tell us about your job.

DORIS: Well, I like my job. It's very interesting. I show people the beautiful things in the museum. For example, there are many old paintings by famous artists. I tell people about the paintings.

SUSAN: Do you like art?

DORIS: Yes, I do. Art is my favorite subject, and I study it in my free time.

SUSAN: What's this, Doris?

DORIS: This is a painting by Mario Angelini. He's an Italian artist.

SUSAN: And what's that over there?

DORIS: That's a modern sculpture. It doesn't have a title. It's by Richard Lopez. He's an American sculptor.

SUSAN: Well, thank you, Doris. I think this is a wonderful museum. And you're right. The things in the museum are beautiful.

Answer TRUE (T) or FALSE (F).

1. Doris Thurston works at the National Museum of Art.   T   F
2. Doris likes her job, but she doesn't like art.   T   F
3. There are many paintings in the museum.   T   F
4. Mario Angelini is an American artist.   T   F
5. There's a modern sculpture in the museum.   T   F
6. Susan thinks the museum is bad.   T   F

THINK

Work with a classmate or a small group. Ask and answer questions about Franklin, Pennsylvania.

PRONOUNCE: [d], [ð]

day [d]	they [ð]

A. Repeat the words and contrast [d] and [ð].

David	Donald	Edward	Doris	good	bad
this	that	them	father	mother	brother

B. Repeat the sentences.

1. This is a good family.
2. David and Donald are brothers.
3. The father is Edward and the mother is Doris.

4. Is this Donald?
5. Yes. That's Donald.
6. Then this is David.

7. Do you think Doris and Edward like Donald and David?
8. I think they do.
9. Yes, they do. They like them.

C. On a sheet of paper, write *a* for the sound [d] and *b* for the sound [ð].

1. old
2. difficult
3. this
4. good
5. mother

6. day
7. brother
8. London
9. they're
10. the

CONVERSATION

Talking at a Party

PHILIP: This is a great party.

VANH: Yes, it is.

PHILIP: Who's that?

VANH: I'm not sure. I think he's in the band.

PHILIP: And who's that?

VANH: That's Lynn's sister. Her name is

Diane.

PHILIP: Does she sing with the band?

VANH: No, she doesn't. She plays the piano.

PHILIP: Who sings?

VANH: I don't know.

INTERACTION

A. Make sentences like the models. Use the cues.

EX. that?
    he's in the band.

    ◻ **Who's that?**
    I'm not sure. I think he's in the band.

1. that?
    she sings with the band.

    ◻

2. that over there?
    he's a student.

    ◻

3. that?
    she works at the hospital.

    ◻

4. that over there?
    he plays the piano.

    ◻

B. Make sentences like the models. Use the cues.

EX. that?
    Lynn's sister/Diane.

    ◻ **Who's that?**
    That's Lynn's sister. Her name is Diane.

    that over there?
    my brother/Jim.

    ◻ **Who's that over there?**
    That's my brother. His name is Jim.

1. that over there?
    Helen's husband/Jack.

    ◻

2. that?
    Carlos's sister/Maria.

    ◻

3. that over there?
    Lynn's brother/David.

    ◻

4. that?
    my cousin/Linda.

    ◻

STUDY 1

Possessive adjectives: *Her name is Diane.*

Notice the possessive forms.

	my your his her its our your their	brother.			my your his her its our your their	brothers.
This is			These are		

Possessive forms change for each person.

I	**my**		we	**our**
you	**your**		you	**your**
he	**his**		they	**their**
she	**her**			
it	**its**			

They do not change for plural nouns.

This is **my** brother.
These are **my** brother**s**.

PRACTICE

A. Look at the pictures and complete the sentences.

EX. This is __**my**__ piano.

1. The cat wants _____ milk.

2. I like _____ shoes.

3. We like _____ houses.

4. I like _____ camera.

5. You have _____ coats.

B. Make sentences with the same meaning, using the possessive.

EX. He has blue eyes.
  ⇨ **His eyes are blue.**

1. She has a beautiful house.
  ⇨

2. I have an old car.
  ⇨

3. It has big eyes.
  ⇨

4. You have a good watch.
  ⇨

5. They have nice friends.
  ⇨

6. We have a new teacher.
  ⇨

STUDY 2

Possessive forms of nouns: *That's Lynn's sister.*

Notice the singular possessive.

This is
| the girl's
John's
Lynn's
the child's |
friend.

These are
| the girl's
John's
Lynn's
the child's |
friends.

Add **'s** to form the possessive of **all** singular nouns.

Notice the plural possessive.

This is | the girls' | friend.

These are | the doctors' | friends.

This is | the children's | friend.

These are | the women's | friends.

Add **'** to form the possessive of plural nouns that end in **s**.
Add **'s** to form the possessive of plural nouns that do not end in **s**.

PRACTICE

A. Identify the objects and the owners in the pictures. Make sentences like the models.

Lynn

pants

John

EX.   ▷ **This is Lynn's piano.**   ▷ **These are John's pants.**

men

dress

Julia

1. ▷   2. ▷

Jack

student

3. ▷   4. ▷

David

Carolyn

5. ▷   6. ▷

B. Identify the objects and the owners. Make sentences like the models.

Jack

Helen

EX. <u>These are Jack's friends</u>.
<u>His friends are</u> nice.

<u>This is Helen's camera</u>.
<u>Her camera is</u> new.

Mary

1. _____ .
_____ big.

Yoko

2. _____ .
_____ beautiful.

Donald

3. _____ .
_____ black.

Mrs. Thurston

4. _____ .
_____ young.

children

5. _____ .
_____ colorful.

George and Wanda

6. _____ .
_____ old.

STUDY 3

Pronunciation of possessives: *John's, Robert's, Alice's*

1. Pronounce **'s** [z] after all vowel sounds and all voiced final consonants [b, n, and so on] except those in group 3 below.

John	John's
Mary	Mary's

2. Pronounce **'s** [s] after the voiceless final sounds [p, t, k].

Robert	Robert's
Philip	Philip's

3. Pronounce **'s** [iz] after the final sounds [s, z, š, ž, č, ǰ].

Alice	Alice's
the coach	the coach's
the judge	the judge's

Possessives of both singular and plural nouns are pronounced like the plurals of nouns.

Pronounce

the mechanic's	like	the mechanics.
the coach's		the coaches.
the worker's		the workers.
the girls'		the girls.

PRACTICE

Pronounce the possessive.

EX. John has a book.
  ▷ **It's John's book.**

1. Philip has a dictionary.
  ▷

2. Alice is writing a letter.
  ▷

3. Dennis has a pen.
  ▷

4. Carolyn has a cat.
  ▷

5. Jack has a car.
  ▷

6. Barbara is drinking tea.
  ▷

7. Lynn is playing the guitar.
  ▷

8. The judge has a problem.
  ▷

9. The coach is playing with a basketball.
  ▷

10. Make your own sentences.
  ▷

STUDY 4

Subject questions: *Who sings with the band?*

Who's that?
That's **Lynn's sister**.

Who plays the piano?
Diane plays the piano.

What is on the chair?
The **guitar** is on the chair.

What is cooking?
The **soup** is cooking.

Use **who** for people. Use **what** for things.

PRACTICE

Read each answer and then ask the question.

EX. Who lives in London_____?
Bill lives in London.

Bill   London

What is on the table_____?
The milk is on the table.

1. _____?
   Alice wants soda.

2. _____?
   The cat is on the table.

3. _____?
   Helen and Jack need money.

4. _____?
   Lynn is playing basketball.

5. _____?
   The coffee is hot.

6. _____?
   David works in New York.

LISTEN

A. Listen and write the conversation.

1. _____ ?
2. _____ . _____ .
3. _____ ?
4. _____ . _____ .
5. _____ .
6. _____ . _____ .
7. _____ .
8. _____ .

B. Look at the pictures below. Then listen to each sentence and write the letter of the sentence next to the matching picture.

1. _____

2. _____

3. _____

4. _____

5. _____

6. _____

SPEAK

A. Listen to the two conversations.

1.   LYNN: This is an interesting party.
    PHILIP: Yes, it is.
    LYNN: Who's that?
    PHILIP: That's Tina. She's a translator.
    LYNN: What's her last name?
    PHILIP: Brown.

2.   LYNN: Is this your coat?
    PHILIP: No, it isn't. I think it's Donald's coat.
    LYNN: Excuse me, Donald. Is this your coat?
    DONALD: Yes, it is. Thank you very much.

B. Practice the conversations with two classmates. Use your own information.

1. STUDENT 1:   This is an interesting party.
   STUDENT 2:   Yes, it is.
   STUDENT 1:   Who's that?
   STUDENT 2:   That's _____. She (He)'s _____.
   STUDENT 1:   What's her (his) last name?
   STUDENT 2:   _____.

2. STUDENT 1:   Is this your _____?
   STUDENT 2:   No, it isn't. I think it's _____'s
                     _____.
   STUDENT 1:   Excuse me, _____. Is this your
                     _____?
   STUDENT 3:   Yes, it is. Thank you very much.

C. Now close your book and practice the conversations with two different classmates.

READ

Carlos, Philip, Lynn, Donald, Vanh, and Mary are at Carolyn Jackson's party. Carolyn is their teacher, and the party is at her house. Carolyn likes big parties. There are twenty people at her house. Carolyn's boyfriend is at the party, too. His name is Charles.

The party is great. The music is good, and Carolyn's food is excellent. Everyone is having a good time. Mary is playing the piano, and Carlos is playing the guitar. Carolyn, Vanh, Donald, and Lynn are singing. Philip doesn't sing very well. He is talking to Charles.

Answer the questions.

1. Who is at Carolyn's party?
2. Who is Carolyn?
3. Who is Charles?
4. Who likes big parties?
5. Where is the party?
6. Are there many people at the party?

Ask your own questions about the second paragraph.

THINK

A. Describe the pictures.

Sylvia Edith

Sylvia and her mother Edith are at home.

Mr. Smith Mr. Ogawa

Mr. Smith and Mr. Ogawa are leaving a restaurant.

B. Ask and answer questions about the pictures.

Richard and Ted are friends.

A man and a woman are on Main Street.

PRONOUNCE: [č]

chin	exploded with friction between tongue and upper gum, voiceless
	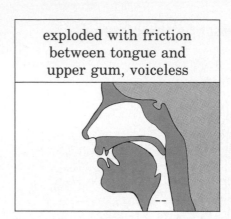

A. Repeat the words.

chin   teacher   **Charles**   **French**   **Chile**   beach

B. Repeat the sentences.

1. Charles is a teacher.
2. He teaches French.
3. He teaches in Chile.
4. Chile has beautiful beaches.
5. There are children at the beach.
6. Charles is the children's teacher.

C. On a sheet of paper, write the number of the words that have the sound [č].

1. change   3. she   5. Chile   7. child   9. children
2. teacher   4. French   6. wash   8. watch   10. fast

KEY TO PRONUNCIATION

Vowels and Diphthongs

[iy]   sheep
[i]   ship
[ey]   pain
[e]   net
[æ]   pan, man
[a]   father, socks
[ow]   phone
[ɔ]   Paul, all
[uw]   pool, two
[u]   foot, pull
[ə́]   nut
[ə]   across

[ay]   buy, eye
[aw]   mouth
[ɔy]   boy

Consonants

VOICELESS		VOICED	
[pʰ]	pan	[b]	band
[tʰ]	tan	[d]	day
[kʰ]	can	[g]	good
[f]	fan	[v]	van
[θ]	three, ether	[ð]	they, either
[s]	sip	[z]	zip
[š]	shin	[ž]	leisure
[č]	chin	[ǰ]	jam
[p]	nap	[l]	light
[t]	bat	[r]	right
[k]	back	[m]	some
		[n]	sun
		[ŋ]	sung

Semiconsonants

[y]   yam, yes
[w]   wood
[h]   hood, he

Syllabic Consonants

[l̥]   apple
[m̥]   stop 'em (stop them)
[n̥]   didn't

Stress and Intonation

Syllable stress (within a word):

Phrase or sentence stress: —•—

Intonation levels
    4 extra high
    3 high
    2 mid
    1 low

Endings for intonation levels

    rise

    sustain

    fade out

Examples of stress and intonation

    yes-no question   Is he home?

    information question   Where is he?

    statement   He's sleeping.

    with emphasis   He's still sleeping!

VOCABULARY

These are words introduced in Student Book 1. The number after each word indicates the page on which it first appears. If a word can be used as more than one part of speech, the way it is used in the text is indicated as follows: n = noun, v = verb, inf = infinitive, prep = preposition, adj = adjective, adv = adverb. Irregular verb forms are indicated as past = past tense. Irregular plural nouns are indicated as pl = plural.

a, 1
about, 15
absent, 7
after, 117
afternoon, 65
all, 117
also, 106
am, 18
an, 59
and, 15
answer (n), 96
answer (v), 94
apple, 59
are, 15
aren't (are not), 88
arm, 146
art, 62
article, 63
artist, 158
ask, 78
at, 55
auto, 110

banana, 99
band, 161
bank, 142
baseball, 118
basement, 88
basket, 150
basketball, 169
be, 18
beach, 176
beautiful, 18
bed, 49
bedroom, 85
big, 46
black, 99
blue, 99
body, 146
book, 56

bookkeeper, 111
boy, 56
boyfriend, 174
box, 150
bread, 127
briefcase, 59
brother, 15
brown, 99
bus, 56
business, 122
busy, 68
but, 120
buy, 100
by, 83

cake, 131
calendar, 119
call (v), 69
camera, 53
capital, 67
car, 83
cat, 103
chair, 84
change (v), 116
chemistry, 63
chicken, 132
child, 147
children, 147
chin, 146
church, 159
city, 24
class, 6
classmate, 2
clearly, 83
clock, 98
close (v), 95
clothes, 113
cloud, 103
club, 113
coach (n), 168

coat, 100
coffee, 76
college, 106
color, 99
colorful, 167
come, 137
computer, 66
cook (n), 24
cook (v), 113
country, 46
cousin, 16
cream, 126
cry, 74
culture, 122

dance, 77
day, 109
dear, 30
dictionary, 169
difficult, 26
dinner, 117
dish, 88
do, 69
doctor, 3
does, 116
doesn't (does not), 128
dog, 23
don't (do not), 94
door, 95
down, 117
Dr., 12
dress (n), 166
drink (v), 75
drive, 100
dry (v), 88

ear, 146
easy, 26
eat, 71
egg, 59

INDEX